Designing Gestural Interfaces

Designing Gestural Interfaces

Dan Saffer

O'REILLY®

Beijing · Cambridge · Farnham · Köln · Sebastopol · Taipei · Tokyo

Designing Gestural Interfaces
by Dan Saffer

Published by O'Reilly Media, Inc., 1005 Gravenstein Highway North, Sebastopol, CA 95472.

O'Reilly books may be purchased for educational, business, or sales promotional use. Online editions are also available for most titles (safari.oreilly.com). For more information, contact our corporate/institutional sales department: (800) 998-9938 or corporate@oreilly.com.

Editor: Mary Treseler

Production Editor: Rachel Monaghan

Copyeditor: Audrey Doyle

Proofreader: Katie Nopper DePasquale

Indexer: Julie Hawks

Cover Designer: Karen Montgomery

Interior Designer: Ron Bilodeau

Illustrator: Jessamyn Read

Printing History:

November 2008: First Edition.

ISBN: 978-0-596-51839-4

[F]

For Rachael, who always gestures in the right direction

Contents

Chapter 8   The Future of Interactive Gestures....... 155

Appendix   A Palette of Human Gestures and Movements 179

Preface

For the past several years, I've been learning to play the cello. As any adult who has ever tried to learn a musical instrument—especially a fretless stringed instrument—can tell you, it's painfully hard. You feel like you don't really know your body at all: your muscles get sore in odd places, you develop strange calluses on your fingers, and you perform stretches with your hands you never thought possible. It requires almost all of your concentration simply to coax the instrument into making a pleasing sound, which is very different from actually making music.

But, ah, when you do begin to make music, it is a thing of joy. When you are able to get a sweet sound with emotional resonance from an inanimate object using only your body, it is an amazing feeling. Gestures create meaning.

That's what this book is about.

Technological, social, and market forces have converged to create a fertile new ground for designers and engineers to plow. The price of processing speed has dropped and sensors are readily available. Touchscreens on our mobile devices, ATMs, and airline check-in kiosks have taught us to expect to be able to manipulate things on-screen with our hands. Games have shown us we can make gestures in space to control objects on-screen. Public restrooms are, believe it or not, test laboratories for interactive gestures: placing your hands under a faucet to turn it on, waving your hands to get a paper towel, stepping into a room to turn on the lights.

All of these things have ushered in a new era of interaction design, one where gestures on a surface and in the air replace (or at least supplement) keyboards, mice, and styli. This new era, however, means those who design and develop more "traditional" systems need to grow their skills, adding in knowledge about kinesiology, sensors, ergonomics, physical computing, touchscreen technology, and new interface patterns.

That's what this book is about.

I wrote this book because, on my third gestural interface project, I was frustrated that I could find only bits and pieces of information about a subject—this subject—that was obviously important and growing rapidly. Why wasn't there a book about these things? I groused. How come I have no idea how big a touchscreen button needs to be? What is a capacitive touchscreen? What kinds of gestures can I use? And thus the idea for the book you are reading was born.

Aside from the constraints of the human body, many of the other parts of this book were changing even as I wrote about them, and new products that utilized interactive gestures seemingly came out every week, if not several times a week, over the course of the nine months I wrote this book (November 2007–July 2008). The newness of the subject was glaringly apparent, but I have tried, when and where possible, to emphasize what is unlikely to change and techniques that are, if not proven, at least being used by practicing designers and developers in the field today.

WHO SHOULD READ THIS BOOK

This book is mostly for interaction and industrial designers who have found themselves in the same position I found myself in several years ago: being asked to design gestural interfaces (especially touchscreens) and, coming from the world of web and desktop software or physical products, having no central place to go to for information to get started. I hope this book is a starting place and a reference point.

And even though there isn't a line of code in this book, I also wrote it with developers in mind, knowing full well that they are often the people who have to take what designers dream up and make it real. I hope everyone involved in creating new products that make use of sensors and interactive surfaces will find something of use in these pages.

HOW TO USE THIS BOOK

This book is divided into roughly four parts. Although certainly you can read the book straight through, you don't have to. I recommend that everyone start with Chapters 1 and 2 just to provide a background for what comes later.

The next section, comprising Chapters 3 and 4, is meant to be used as reference material, mostly when you're designing or are in the process of designing. The patterns show how other designers have solved interface challenges in the past.

Chapters 5 through 7 are about the process of design, from documentation to prototyping to communicating what the product does to its audience. You also can use these chapters for reference as necessary.

Chapter 8 takes a look at future trends in this subject—a future that gets closer and closer every day. It was, after all, only six years ago that the gestural interfaces in *Minority Report* were science fiction, and now we can see them being deployed everywhere. "The future is here," as William Gibson famously noted. "It's just not evenly distributed."

Designers can flip through the appendix for inspiration, especially when creating free-form gestural interfaces.

HOW TO CONTACT US

Please address comments and questions concerning this book to the publisher:

O'Reilly Media, Inc.
1005 Gravenstein Highway North
Sebastopol, CA 95472
800-998-9938 (in the U.S. or Canada)
707-829-0515 (international/local)
707-829-0104 (fax)

We have a web page for this book, where we list errata, examples, and any additional information. You can access this page at:

http://www.oreilly.com/catalog/9780596518394

To comment or ask technical questions about this book, send email to:

bookquestions@oreilly.com

For more information about our books, conferences, Resource Centers, and the O'Reilly Network, see our website at:

http://www.oreilly.com

SAFARI® BOOKS ONLINE

 When you see a Safari® Books Online icon on the cover of your favorite technology book, that means the book is available online through the O'Reilly Network Safari Bookshelf.

Safari offers a solution that's better than e-books. It's a virtual library that lets you easily search thousands of top tech books, cut and paste code samples, download chapters, and find quick answers when you need the most accurate, current information. Try it for free at *http://safari.oreilly.com*.

ACKNOWLEDGMENTS

It's easy to come up with an idea for a book, but it's much harder to write one. It's a task that, like most other products, requires lots of people to make it a reality.

This book would not be possible without the patience, support, and 6:00 a.m. writing wake-up calls of my wife, Rachael King. Her encouragement and understanding kept me going on those days when I could eek out only a sentence—which were many.

My daughter Fiona's insistence that I not work on this book and instead play Wii with her also, I'm sure, kept me sane and contributed vastly to the quality of this tome. (At the very least, I got to practice many interactive gestures!)

My family and friends have my undying gratitude for their love, patience, and support throughout this process, especially my parents.

My former colleagues at Adaptive Path fed me a constant diet of new material, both in links to interesting stuff and in projects to work on that constantly expanded what I knew—or needed to know—to make this book as rich as it is.

This book would be boring indeed without the images contained therein, and I'd like to thank the companies that contributed them and the individuals who graciously made their photographs available via Creative Commons licenses for commercial use.

My colleague and friend, Rachel Glaves, created many of the illustrations in the book, and the book is much improved because of it.

My other colleague and friend, Sarah B. Nelson, took the photographs in the appendix and made them look good. My model, Ellen Ho, really brought the gestures to life.

I also benefited greatly from the review of others who read and commented on the manuscript as it was in development. For their advice and expertise, I thank them: Bill DeRouchey, Kevin Arthur, Nathan Moody, Juhan Sonin, Cem Keskin, Chong Lee Khoo, Dan Harrelson, Kate Fitch, and Jennifer Bove.

The contributors to the Interaction Design Association's mailing list and especially to the Interactive Gestures Wiki were an enormous help and source of material and inspiration.

I also want to thank the staff at O'Reilly who took a chance on this book and have supported its development and promotion: Jacque McIlvaine, Marlowe Shaeffer, Katheryn Barrett, Laurel Ackerman, Ron Bilodeau, Rachel Monaghan, Adam Witwer, Audrey Doyle, Jessamyn Read, Tim O'Reilly, and especially my editor, Mary Treseler.

San Francisco, California
November 2008

Introducing Interactive Gestures

> *One of the things our grandchildren will find quaintest about us is that we distinguish the digital from the real.*
>
> —William Gibson in a *Rolling Stone* interview, November 7, 2007

A man wearing special gloves stands in front of a large, translucent screen. He waves his hand in front of it, and objects on the screen move. It's as though he's conducting an orchestra or is some sort of high-tech sorcerer's apprentice, making objects fly about with just a sweep of his arm. He makes another gesture, and a video begins to play. With both hands, he stretches the video to a larger size, filling more of the screen. It's like magic.

Another place, another time: a different man stands in front of an audience. He's running his fingers over a table-size touchscreen before him as though he is a keyboard player in a rock band, his fingers rapidly manipulating images on the screen by dragging them around. He's making lines appear on-screen with his fingers and turning them into silky, ink-like paintings. He's playing, really—showing off. He drags his fingers across the surface and leaves a trail of bubbles. It's also like magic.

The first man doesn't really exist, although you'd probably recognize the actor playing him: Tom Cruise. The scene is from the movie *Minority Report* (2002), and it gave the general public its first look at a computer that responds to gestures instead of to speech, a keyboard, or a mouse. It was an impressive feat of visual effects, and it made a huge impression on people everywhere, especially interaction designers, some of whom had been working on or thinking about similar systems for years.

The second man does exist, and his name is Jeff Han. Not only did his jumbo touchscreen devices influence *Minority Report*, but his live demonstrations—first privately and then publicly at the 2006 TED conference[*]—will likely go down in computer history near the "Mother of All Demos" presentation that Doug Engelbart made in 1968, in which he showed now-familiar idioms such as

---

[*] Watch the demo yourself at *http://www.ted.com/index.php/talks/view/id/65*.

email, hypertext, and the mouse. Han's demos sparked thousands of conversations, blog posts, emails, and commentary.

Figure 1-1. *Jeff Han demos a multitouch touchscreen at the 2006 TED conference. Since then, Han has created Perceptive Pixel, a company that produces these devices for high-end clients. Courtesy TED Conferences, LLC.*

Since then, consumer electronics manufacturers such as Nintendo, Apple, Nokia, Sony Ericsson, LG, and Microsoft have all released products that are controlled using interactive gestures. Within the next several years, it's not an exaggeration to say that hundreds of millions of devices will have gestural interfaces. A **gesture**, for the purposes of this book, is any physical movement that a digital system can sense and respond to without the aid of a traditional pointing device such as a mouse or stylus. A wave, a head nod, a touch, a toe tap, and even a raised eyebrow can be a gesture.

In addition to touchscreen kiosks that populate our airports and execute our banking as ATMs, the most famous of the recent products that use gestures are Nintendo's Wii and Apple's iPhone and iPod Touch. The Wii has a set of wireless controllers that users hold to play its games. Players make movements in space that are then reflected in some way on-screen. The iPhone and iPod Touch are devices that users control via touching the screen, manipulating digital objects with a tap of a fingertip.

Figure 1-2. *Rather than focusing on the technical specs of the gaming console like their competitors, Nintendo designers and engineers focused on the controllers and the gaming experience, creating the Wii, a compelling system that uses gestures to control on-screen avatars. Courtesy Nintendo.*

TAP IS THE NEW CLICK

We've entered a new era of interaction design. For the past 40 years, we have been using the same human-computer interaction paradigms that were designed by the likes of Doug Engelbart, Alan Kay, Tim Mott, Larry Tesler, and others at Xerox PARC in the 1960s and 1970s. Cut and paste. Save. Windows. The desktop metaphor. And so many others that we now don't even think about when working on our digital devices. These interaction conventions will continue, of course, but they will also be supplemented by many others that take advantage of the whole human body, of sensors, of new input devices, and of increased processing power.

We've entered the era of interactive gestures.

The next several years will be seminal years for interaction designers and engineers who will create the next generation of interaction design inputs, possibly defining them for decades to come. We will design new ways of interacting with our devices, environment, and even each other. We have an opportunity that comes along only once in a generation, and we should seize it. How we can create this new era of interactive gestures is what this book is about.

Currently, most gestural interfaces can be categorized as either **touchscreen** or **free-form**. Touchscreen gestural interfaces—or, as some call them, touch user interfaces (TUIs)—require the user to be touching the device directly. This puts a constraint on the types of gestures that can be used to control it. Free-form gestural interfaces don't require the user to touch or handle them directly. Sometimes a controller or glove is used as an input device, but even more often (and increasingly so) the body is the only input device for free-form gestural interfaces.

Our relationship to our digital technology is only going to get more complicated as time goes on. Users, especially sophisticated users, are slowly being trained to expect that devices and appliances will have touchscreens and/or will be manipulated by gestures. But it's not just early adopters: even the general public is being exposed to more and more touchscreens via airport and retail kiosks and voting machines, and these users are discovering how easy and enjoyable they are to use.

DIRECT VERSUS INDIRECT MANIPULATION

The ease of use one experiences with a well-designed touchscreen comes from what University of Maryland professor Ben Shneiderman coined as **direct manipulation** in a seminal 1983 paper. Direct manipulation is the ability to manipulate digital objects on a screen without the use of command-line commands—for example, dragging a file to a trash can on your desktop instead of typing **del** into a command line. As it was 1983, Shneiderman was mostly talking about mice, joysticks, and other input devices, as well as then-new innovations such as the desktop metaphor.

Touchscreens and gestural interfaces take direct manipulation to another level. Now, users can simply touch the item they want to manipulate right on the screen itself, moving it, making it bigger, scrolling it, and so on. This is the ultimate in direct manipulation: using the body to control the digital (and sometimes even the physical) space around us. Of course, as we'll discuss in Chapter 4, there are indirect manipulations with gestural interfaces as well. One simple example is The Clapper.

Shneiderman, Ben. "Direct Manipulation: A Step Beyond Programming Languages." *IEEE Computer* 16(8): 57–69, August 1983.

Figure 1-3. *The Clapper turns ordinary rooms into interactive environments. Occupants use indirect manipulation in the form of a clap to control analog objects in the room. Courtesy Joseph Enterprises.*

The Clapper was one of the first consumer devices sold with an auditory sensor.* It plugs into an electrical socket, and then other electronics are plugged into it. You clap your hands to turn the electrical flow off (or on), effectively turning off (or on) whatever is plugged into The Clapper. It allows users indirect control over their physical environment via an interactive gesture: a clap.

This use of the whole body, however, can be seen as the more natural state of user interfaces. (Indeed, some call interactive gestures natural user interfaces [NUIs].) One could argue, in fact, that the current "traditional" computing arrangement of keyboard, mouse, and monitor goes against thousands of years of biology. As a 1993 *Wired* article on Stanford professor David Liddle notes:[†]

“ *We're using bodies evolved for hunting, gathering, and gratuitous violence for information-age tasks like word processing and spreadsheet tweaking. And gratuitous violence.*

“ *Humans are born with a tool kit at least 15,000 years old. So, Liddle asks, if the tool kit was designed for foraging and mammoth trapping, why not try to make the tasks we do with our machines today look like the tasks the body was designed for? 'The most nearly muscular mentality that we use (in computation) is pointing with a mouse,' Liddle says. 'We use such a tiny part of our repertoire of sound and motion and vision in any interaction with an electronic system. In retrospect, that seems strange and not very obvious why it should be that way.'*

“ *Human beings possess a wide variety of physical skills—we can catch baseballs, dodge projectiles, climb trees—which all have a sort of 'underlying computational power' about them. But we rarely take*

---

* The Clapper also had an iconic commercial with an extremely catchy jingle: "Clap on! Clap off!" See the commercial and watch The Clapper in action at *http://www.youtube.com/watch?v=WsxcdVbE3mI.*

† "Dogs Don't Do Math," by Tom Bestor, November 1993. Found online at *http://www.wired.com/wired/archive/1.05/dogs.html.*

advantage of these abilities because they have little evolutionary value now that we're firmly ensconced as the food chain's top seed. »

Fifteen years after Liddle noted this, it's finally changing.

A BRIEF HISTORY OF GESTURAL INTERFACES

Figure 1-4. *How the computer sees us. With traditional interfaces, humans are reduced to an eye and a finger. Gestural interfaces allow for fuller use of the human body to trigger system responses. Courtesy Dan O'Sullivan and Tom Igoe.*

Figure 1-5. *If you don't need a keyboard, mouse, or screen, you don't need much of an interface either. You activate this faucet by putting your hands beneath it. Of course, this can lead to confusion. If there are no visible controls, how do you know how to even turn the faucet on? Courtesy Sloan Valve Company.*

As The Clapper illustrates, gestural interfaces are really nothing new. In one sense, everything we do with digital devices requires some sort of physical action to create a digital response. You press a key, and a letter or number appears on-screen. You move a mouse, and a pointer scurries across the screen.

What is different, though, between gestural interfaces and traditional interfaces is simply this: gestural interfaces have a much wider range of actions with which to manipulate a system. In addition to being able to type, scroll, point and click, and perform all the other standard interactions available to desktop systems,* gestural interfaces can take advantage of the whole body for triggering system behaviors. The flick of a finger can start a scroll. The twist of a hand can transform an image. The sweep of an arm can clear a screen. A person entering a room can change the temperature.

Removing the constraints of the keyboard-controller-screen setup of most mobile devices and desktop/ laptop computers allows devices employing interactive gestures to take many forms. Indeed, the form of a "device" can be a physical object that

---

* This has some notable exceptions. See later in this chapter.

is usually analog/mechanical. Most touchscreens are like this, appearing as normal screens or even, in the case of the iPhone and iPod Touch, as slabs of black glass. And the "interface"? Sometimes all but invisible. Take, for instance, the motion-activated sinks now found in many public restrooms. The interface for them is typically a small sensor hidden below the faucet that, when detecting movement in the sink (e.g., someone putting her hands into the sink), triggers the system to turn the water on (or off).

Computer scientists and human-computer interaction advocates have been talking about this kind of "embodied interaction" for at least the past two decades. Paul Dourish in his book *Where the Action Is* captured the vision well:

> " *By embodiment, I don't mean simply physical reality, but rather, the way that physical and social phenomena unfold in real time and real space as a part of the world in which we are situated, right alongside and around us…Interacting in the world, participating in it and acting through it, in the absorbed and unreflective manner of normal experience.* "

As sensors and microprocessors have become faster, smaller, and cheaper, reality has started to catch up with the vision, although we still have quite a way to go.

Of course, it hasn't happened all at once. Samuel C. Hurst created the first touch device in 1971, dubbed the Elograph.[*] By 1974, Hurst and his new company, Elographics, had developed five-wire resistive technology, which is still one of the most popular touchscreen technologies used today. In 1977, Elographics, backed by Siemens, created Accutouch, the first true touchscreen device. Accutouch was basically a curved glass sensor that became increasingly refined over the next decade.

Figure 1-6. *The Accutouch, the first real "touchscreen." Courtesy Elo TouchSystems.*

---

[*] See *http://www.elotouch.com/AboutElo/History/* for a detailed history of the Elograph.

Myron Krueger created in the late 1970s what could rightly be called the first indirect manipulation interactive gesture system, dubbed VIDEOPLACE. VIDEO-PLACE (which could be a wall or a desk) was a system of projectors, video cameras, and other hardware that enabled users to interact using a rich set of gestures without the use of special gloves, mice, or styli.

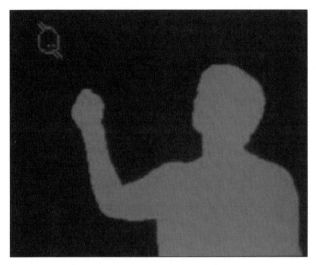

Figure 1-7. *In VIDEOPLACE, users in separate rooms were able to interact with one another and with digital objects. Video cameras recorded users' movements, then analyzed and transferred them to silhouette representations projected on a wall or screen. The sense of presence was such that users actually jumped back when their silhouette touched that of other users. Courtesy Matthias Weiss.*

In 1982, Nimish Mehta at the University of Toronto developed what could be the first **multitouch** system, the Flexible Machine Interface, for his master's thesis.[*] Multitouch systems allow users more than one contact point at a time, so you can use two hands to manipulate objects on-screen or touch two or more places on-screen simultaneously. The Flexible Machine Interface combined finger pressure with simple image processing to create some very basic picture drawing and other graphical manipulation.

Outside academia, the 1980s found touchscreens making their way to the public first (as most new technology does) in commercial and industrial use, particularly in point-of-sale (POS) devices in restaurants, bars, and retail environments. Currently, touchscreen POS devices have penetrated more than 90% of food and beverage establishments in the United States.[†]

---

[*] Mehta, Nimish. "A Flexible Machine Interface." M.A.Sc. thesis, Department of Electrical Engineering, University of Toronto, 1982. Supervised by Professor K.C. Smith.

[†] According to *The Professional Bar and Beverage Manager's Handbook*, by Amanda Miron and Douglas Robert Brown (Atlantic Publishing Company).

Figure 1-8. *A POS touchscreen. According to the National Restaurant Association, touchscreen POS systems pay for themselves in savings to the establishment. Courtesy GVISION USA, Inc.*

The Hewlett-Packard 150 was probably the first computer sold for personal use that incorporated touch. Users could touch the screen to position the cursor or select on-screen buttons, but the touch targets (see later in this chapter) were fairly primitive, allowing for only approximate positioning.

Figure 1-9. *Released in 1983, the HP 150 didn't have a traditional touchscreen, but a monitor surrounded by a series of vertical and horizontal infrared light beams that crossed just in front of the screen, creating a grid. If a user's finger touched the screen and broke one of the lines, the system would position the cursor at (or more likely near) the desired location, or else activate a soft function key. Courtesy Hewlett-Packard.*

At Rank EuroPARC, Pierre Wellner designed the Digital Desk in the early 1990s.[*] The Digital Desk used video cameras and a projector to project a digital surface onto a physical desk, which users could then manipulate with their hands.[†] Notably, the Digital Desk was the first to use some of the emerging patterns of interactive gestures such as *Pinch to Shrink* (see Chapter 3).

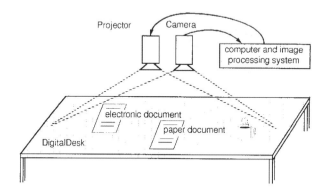

Figure 1-10. *A diagram of the Digital Desk system.*

Figure 1-11. *Simon, released in 1994, was the first mobile touchscreen device. It suffered from some serious design flaws, such as not being able to show more than a few keyboard keys simultaneously, but it was a decade ahead of its time. Courtesy IBM.*

More than a decade before Apple released the iPhone (and other handset manufacturers such as LG, Sony Ericsson, and Nokia released similar touchscreen phones as well), IBM and Bell South launched Simon, a touchscreen mobile phone. It was ahead of its time and never caught on, but it demonstrated that a mobile touchscreen could be manufactured and sold.

In the late 1990s and the early 2000s, touchscreens began to make their way into wide public use via retail kiosks, public information displays, airport check-in services, transportation ticketing systems, and new ATMs.

---

[*] Wellner, Pierre. "The DigitalDesk Calculator: Tactile Manipulation on a Desktop Display." Proceedings of the Fourth Annual Symposium on User Interface Software and Technology (UIST): 27–33, 1991.

[†] Watch the video demonstration at *http://video.google.com/videoplay?docid=5772530828816089246.*

Figure 1-12. *Antenna Design's award-winning self-service check-in kiosk for JetBlue Airlines. Courtesy JetBlue and Antenna Design.*

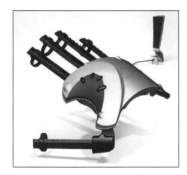

Figure 1-13. *The Essential Reality P5 Glove is likely the first commercial controller for gestural interfaces, for use with the game Black & White. Courtesy Lionhead Studios.*

Lionhead Studios released what is likely the first home gaming gestural interface system in 2001 with its game, Black & White. A player controlled the game via a special glove that, as the player gestured physically, would be mimicked by a digital hand on-screen. In arcades in 2001, Konami's MoCap Boxing game had players put on boxing gloves and stand in a special area monitored with infrared motion detectors, then "box" opponents by making movements that actual boxers would make.

The mid-2000s have simply seen the arrival of gestural interfaces for the mass market. In 2006, Nintendo released its Wii gaming system. In 2007, to much acclaim, Apple launched its iPhone and iPod Touch, which were the first touchscreen devices to receive widespread media attention and television advertising demonstrating their touchscreen capabilities. In 2008, handset manufacturers such as LG, Sony Ericsson, and Nokia released their own touchscreen mobile devices. Also in 2008, Microsoft launched MS Surface, a large, table-like touchscreen that is used in commercial spaces for gaming and retail display. And Jeff Han now manufactures his giant touchscreens for government agencies and large media companies such as CNN.

GEEKY STUFF YOU MIGHT CARE ABOUT

What's the Deal with Interactive Gestures and Public Restrooms?

If you have visited a public bathroom in the past several years, you've likely encountered interactive gestures that control everything from washing your hands to flushing the toilet. What gives? Why have trips to the bathroom become visits to interaction design labs?

There are a few possible reasons. The first is that bathrooms are places where bacteria live, and people have grown increasingly hesitant to touch things there. Thus, gestures allow us to interact with the environment without requiring much physical contact.

The second reason is simply one of maintenance and conservation. Bathrooms require a lot of upkeep, and having toilets automatically flush, paper towels dispense only a small amount, and sinks automatically shut off saves both maintenance and resources (read: money).

The third reason is one of human nature. As Arthur C. Clarke noted, "Any sufficiently advanced technology is indistinguishable from magic," and interactive gestures are quite magical right now. And we may need magic in our bathrooms—they can be places of anxiety and discomfort. Anthropologist Bronislaw Malinowski in his "Theory of the Gap" claimed that humans used magic to reduce anxiety, to overcome unpredictability and uncertainty. So, perhaps it makes perfect sense to have magic in our bathrooms.

Whatever the reason, public restrooms are the new labs for interactive gestures.

The future (see Chapter 8) should be interesting.

THE MECHANICS OF TOUCHSCREENS AND GESTURAL CONTROLLERS

Even though forms of gestural devices can vary wildly—from massive touch-screens to invisible overlays onto environments—every device or environment that employs gestures to control it has at least three general parts: a **sensor**, a **comparator**, and an **actuator**. These three parts can be a single physical component, or, more typically, multiple components of any gestural system, such as a motion detector (a sensor), a computer (the comparator), and a motor (the actuator).

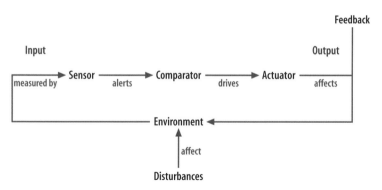

Figure 1-14. *The basic components of any gestural system*

A **sensor** is typically an electrical or electronic component whose job is to detect changes in the environment. These changes can be any number of things, depending on the type of sensor, of which there are many.[*] The most common types currently used for interactive gestures are:

Pressure
> To detect whether something is being pressed or stood on. This is often mechanical in nature.

Light
> To detect the presence of light sources (also called a *photodetector*). This is used mostly in environments, especially in lighting systems.

Proximity
> To detect the presence of an object in space. This can be done in any number of ways, from infrared sensors to motion and acoustic sensors.

Acoustic
> To detect the presence of sound. Typically, this is done with small microphones.

Tilt
> To detect angle, slope, and elevation. Tilt sensors generate an artificial horizon and then measure the incline with respect to that horizon.

Motion
> To detect movement and speed. Some common sensors use microwave or ultrasonic pulses that measure when a pulse bounces off a moving object (which is how radar guns catch you speeding).

---

[*] *http://en.wikipedia.org/wiki/Sensor* has a more complete list, including many sensors that are currently used only for scientific or industrial applications.

Orientation

To detect position and direction. These are often used in navigation systems currently, but position within environments could become increasingly important and would need to be captured by cameras, triangulating proximity sensors, or even GPSes in the case of large-scale use.

It's no exaggeration to state that the type of sensor you employ entirely determines the types of gestural interactions that are possible. If the system can't detect what a user is doing, those gestures might as well not be happening. I can wave at my laptop as much as I want, but if it doesn't have any way to detect my motion, I simply look like an idiot.

It is crucially important to calibrate the sensitivity of the sensor (or the moderation of the comparator). A sensor that is too sensitive will trigger too often and, perhaps, too rapidly for humans to react to. A sensor that is too dull will not respond quickly enough, and the system will seem sluggish or nonresponsive.

The size (for touchscreens) or coverage area of the sensor is also very important, as it determines what kinds of gestures (broad or small, one or two hands, etc.) are appropriate or even possible to have.

 The larger the sensor coverage area is, the broader the gesture possible.

Often in more complex systems, multiple sensors will work together to allow for more nuanced movement and complicated gesture combinations. (To have 3D gestures, multiple sensors are a necessity to get the correct depth.) Many Apple products (including Apple laptops) have accelerometers to detect speed and motion built into them, as do Wii controllers. But accelerometers are tuned to themselves, not to the environment, so they alone can't determine the user's position in the room or the direction the user is facing, only whether the device is moving and the direction and speed at which it is moving. For orientation within an environment or sophisticated detection of angles, other sensors need to be deployed. The Wii, for instance, deploys both accelerometers and gyroscopes within its controllers for tilt and motion detection, and an infrared sensor that communicates to the "sensor bar" to indicate orientation* for a much wider range of possible gestures.

---

* See "At the Heart of the Wii Micron-Size Machines," by Michel Marriott, in *The New York Times*, December 21, 2006; *http://www.nytimes.com/2006/12/21/technology/21howw.html?partner=permalink&exprod=permalink*.

GEEKY STUFF YOU MIGHT CARE ABOUT

Touch Events and Touchscreen Sensors

A **touch event** is the technical term for when a touchscreen system knows that a user has touched the screen. Touch events are a combination of the sensor and the comparator, but the technology the system uses to detect a touch varies.

In most modern touchscreen interfaces, the sensor is a touch-responsive glass panel that usually employs one of three technologies: resistive, surface wave, or capacitive. *Resistive systems* are made up of two layers. When a user touches the top layer, the two layers press together, triggering a touch event. Because of how resistive systems work, they require pressure (and can measure it well), but multitouch does not work very well (if at all). *Surface wave systems* generate ultrasonic waves. When a user touches the screen, a portion of the wave is absorbed, and that registers as a touch event. *Capacitive sensor panels* are coated with a material that stores electrical charge. When a user touches the screen (or, in some cases, even hovers over the screen), a portion of the charge is transferred to the user, decreasing the panel's capacitive layer and thus triggering a touch event.

Another method, particularly for large displays, incorporates *infrared beams* that skim the (flat) surface of a screen in a grid-like matrix. When an object, such as a user's finger, touches the screen, it breaks the beams, and the X and Y positions of the object can be calculated. Sensitivity is determined by how close the beams are to each other.

Infrared light can also be used in *frustrated total internal reflection (FTIR)* and *diffused illumination (DI)* systems, which use infrared cameras to determine touch events, especially multitouch events.[*] With an FTIR setup, an infrared camera is placed below a sheet of Plexiglas and an infrared light is shone into the side of the Plexiglas (most often by shining IR LEDs onto the sides of the acrylic). The light reflects around the inside of the Plexiglas unhindered. But when a finger touches the surface, this light is "frustrated," causing the light to scatter downward where the camera can detect it, resulting in a touch event.

There are two different kinds of DI systems: rear and front, depending on the direction in which the infrared light is being projected. With rear DI, infrared lights shine upward at a clear surface (glass, acrylic, Plexiglas, etc.) from below (i.e., from the rear of the surface). A diffuser (a device that diffuses, spreads out, or scatters light in some manner to create a soft light) is placed on top of or underneath the touch surface. When an object, such as a finger, touches the surface (creating what are known as *blobs*), it reflects more light than the diffuser or objects in the background, and the camera below senses this extra light, creating a touch event. Depending on the diffuser, rear DI can also detect objects hovering over the surface.

Front DI is when the infrared light is projected on top of the surface from above (i.e., from the front). As with rear DI, a diffuser used to soften the light is placed on the top or bottom of the surface. When an object, such as a finger, touches the surface, it makes a shadow in the position of the object that the camera positioned below detects and uses to determine a touch event.

---

[*] For a more detailed view of FTIR and DI systems, read "Getting Started with MultiTouch" at *http://nuigroup.com/forums/viewthread/1982/*.

Once a sensor detects its target, it passes the information on to what is known in systems theory as a **comparator**. The comparator compares the current state to the previous state or the goal of the system and then makes a judgment. For many gestural interfaces, the comparator is a microprocessor running software, which decides what to do about the data coming into the system via the sensor. Certainly, there are all-mechanical systems that work with gestures, but they tend toward cruder on/off scenarios, such as lights that come on when someone walks past them. Only with a microprocessor can you design a system with much nuance, one that can make more sophisticated decisions.

Those decisions get passed on to an **actuator** in the form of a command. Actuators can be analog or mechanical, similar to the way the machinery of The Clapper turns lights on; or they can be digital, similar to the way tilting the iPhone changes its screen orientation from portrait to landscape. With mechanical systems, the actuator is frequently a small electric motor that powers a physical object, such as a motor to open an automatic door. As with the comparator's decision making, for digital systems, it is software that drives the actuator. It is software that determines what happens when a user touches the screen or extends an arm.

Of course, software doesn't design and code itself, and sensors and motors and the like aren't attached randomly to systems. They need to be designed.

DESIGNING INTERACTIVE GESTURES: THE BASICS

The design of any product or service should start with the needs of those who will use it, tempered by the constraints of the environment, technology, resources, and organizational goals, such as business objectives. The needs of users can range from simple (I want to turn on a light) to very complex (I want to fall in love). (Most human experience lies between those two poles, I think.) However natural, interesting, amusing, novel, or innovative an interactive gesture is, if the users' needs aren't met, the design is a failure.

The first question that anyone designing a gestural interface should ask is: should this even be a gestural interface? Simply because we can now do interactive gestures doesn't mean they are appropriate for every situation. As Bill Buxton notes,[*] when it comes to technology, everything is best for something and worse for something else, and interactive gestures are no exception.

There are several reasons to *not* have a gestural interface:

---

[*] See Bill Buxton's multitouch overview at *http://www.billbuxton.com/multitouchOverview.html*.

Heavy data input

Although some users adapt to touchscreen keyboards easily, a keyboard is decidedly faster for most people to use when they are entering text or numbers.

Reliance on the visual

Many gestural interfaces use visual feedback alone to indicate that an action has taken place (such as a button being pressed). In addition, most touchscreens and many gestural systems in general rely entirely on visual displays with little to no haptic affordances or feedback. There is often no physical feeling that a button has been pressed, for instance. If your users are visually impaired (as most adults over a certain age are) a gestural interface may not be appropriate.

Reliance on the physical

Likewise, gestural interfaces can be more physically demanding than a keyboard/screen. The broader and more physical the gesture is (such as a kick, for instance), the more likely that some people won't be able to perform the gesture due to age, infirmity, or simply environmental conditions; pressing touchscreen buttons in winter gloves is difficult, for instance. The inverse is also true: the subtler and smaller the movement, the less likely everyone will be able to perform it. The keyboard on the iPhone, for instance, is entirely too small and delicate to be used by anyone whose fingers are large or otherwise not nimble.

Inappropriate for context

The environment can be nonconducive to a gestural interface in any number of situations, either due to privacy reasons or simply to avoid embarrassing the system's users. Designers need to take into account the probable environment of use and determine what, if any, kind of gesture will work in that environment.

There are, of course, many reasons to use a gestural interface. Everything that a noninteractive gesture can be used for—communication, manipulating objects, using a tool, making music, and so on—can also be done using an interactive gesture. Gestural interfaces are particularly good for:

More natural interactions

Human beings are physical creatures; we like to interact directly with objects. We're simply wired this way. Interactive gestures allow users to interact naturally with digital objects in a physical way, like we do with physical objects.

Less cumbersome or visible hardware

With many gestural systems, the usual hardware of a keyboard and a mouse isn't necessary: a touchscreen or other sensors allow users to perform actions without this hardware. This benefit allows for gestural interfaces to be put in places where a traditional computer configuration would be impractical or out of place, such as in retail stores, museums, airports, and other public spaces.

Figure 1-15. *New York City in late 2006 installed touchscreens in the back seats of taxicabs. Although clunky, they allow for the display of interactive maps and contextual information that passengers might find useful, such as a Zagat restaurant guide. Courtesy New York City Taxi and Limousine Commission.*

More flexibility

As opposed to fixed, physical buttons, a touchscreen, like all digital displays, can change at will, allowing for many different configurations depending on functionality requirements. Thus, a very small screen (such as those on most consumer electronics devices or appliances) can change buttons as needed. This can have usability issues (see later in this chapter), but the ability to have many controls in a small space can be a huge asset for designers. And with nontouchscreen gestures, the sky is the limit, space-wise. One small sensor, which can be nearly invisible, can detect enough input to control the system. No physical controls or even a screen are required.

More nuance

Keyboards, mice, trackballs, styli, and other input devices, although excellent for many situations, are simply not as able to convey as much subtlety as the human body. A raised eyebrow, a wagging finger, or crossed arms can deliver a wealth of meaning in addition to controlling a tool. Gestural systems have not begun to completely tap the wide emotional palette of humans that they can, and likely will, eventually exploit.

More fun

> You can design a game in which users press a button and an on-screen avatar swings a tennis racket. But it is simply more entertaining—for both players and observers—to mimic swinging a tennis racket physically and see the action mirrored on-screen. Gestural systems encourage play and exploration of a system by providing a more hands-on (sometimes literally hands-on) experience.

Once the decision has been made to have a gestural interface, the next question to answer is what kind of gestural interface it will be: direct, indirect, or hybrid. As I write this, particularly with devices and appliances, the answer will be fairly easy: a direct-manipulation touchscreen is the most frequently employed gestural interface currently. In the future, as an increasing variety of sensors are built into devices and environments, this may change, but for now touchscreens are the new standard for gestural interfaces.

THE CHARACTERISTICS OF GOOD GESTURAL INTERFACES

Although particular aspects of gestural systems require more and different kinds of consideration, the characteristics of a good gestural interface don't differ much from the characteristics of any other well-designed interactive system.[*] Designers often use Liz Sanders' phrase "useful, usable, and desirable"[†] to describe well-designed products, or they say that products should be "intuitive" or "innovative." All of that really means gestural interfaces should be:

Discoverable

> Being discoverable can be a major issue for gestural interfaces. How can you tell whether a screen is touchable? How can you tell whether an environment is interactive? Before we can interact with a gestural system, we have to know one is there and how to begin to interact with it, which is where **affordances** come into play. An affordance is one or multiple properties of an object that give some indication of how to interact with that object or a feature on that object. A button, because of how it moves, has an affordance of pushing. Appearance and texture are the major sources of what psychologist James Gibson called affordances,[‡] popularized in the design community by Don Norman in his seminal 1988 book *The Psychology of Everyday Things* (later renamed *The Design of Everyday Things*).

---

[*] For a longer discussion, see *Designing for Interaction* by Dan Saffer (Peachpit Press): 60–68.

[†] See "Converging Perspectives: Product Development Research for the 1990s," by Liz Sanders, in *Design Management Journal*, 1992.

[‡] Gibson, J.J. "The theory of affordances," in *Perceiving, Acting, and Knowing: Toward an Ecological Psychology*, R. Shaw and J. Bransford (Eds.) (Lawrence Erlbaum): 67–82.

Figure 1-16. *Without the tiny diagrams on the dispenser, there would be no affordances to let you know how to get the toilet paper out. Gestural interfaces need to be discoverable so that they can be used. Courtesy Yu Wei Products Company.*

Trustworthy

Unless they are desperate, before users will engage with a device, the interface needs to look as though it isn't going to steal their money, misuse their personal data, or break down. Gestural interfaces have to appear competent and safe, and they must respect users' privacy (see "The Ethics of Gestures" in Chapter 8). Users are also now suspicious of gestural interfaces and often an **attraction affordance** needs to be employed (see Chapter 7).

Responsive

We're used to instant reaction to physical manipulation of objects. After all, we're usually touching things that don't have a microprocessor and sensor that need to figure out what's going on. Thus, responsiveness is incredibly important. When engaged with a gestural interface, users want to know that the system has heard and understood any commands given to it. This is where **feedback** comes in. Every action by a human directed toward a gestural interface, no matter how slight, should be accompanied by some acknowledgment of the action whenever possible and as rapidly as possible (100 ms or less is ideal as it will feel instantaneous). This can be tricky, as the responsiveness of the system is tied directly to the responsiveness of the system's sensors, and sensors that are too responsive can be even more irksome than those that are dull. Imagine if The Clapper picked up every slight sound and turned the lights on and off, on and off, over and over again! But not having near-immediate feedback can cause errors, some of them potentially serious. Without any response, users will often repeat an action they just performed, such as pushing a button again. Obviously, this can cause problems, such as accidentally buying an item twice or, if the button was connected to dangerous machinery, injury or death. If a response to an action is going to take significant time (more than one second), feedback is required that lets the user know the system has heard the request and is doing something about it. Progress bars are an excellent example of responsive feedback: they don't decrease waiting time, but they make it seem as though they do. They're responsive.

Appropriate

Gestural systems need to be appropriate to the culture, situation, and context they are in. Certain gestures are offensive in certain cultures. An "okay" gesture, commonplace in North America and Western Europe, is insulting in Greece, Turkey, the Middle East, and Russia, for instance.* An overly complicated gestural system that involves waving arms and dancing around in a public place is not likely to be an appropriate system unless it is in a nightclub or other performance space.

Meaningful

The coolest interactive gesture in the world is empty unless it has meaning for the person performing it; which is to say, unless the gestural system meets the needs of those who use it, it is not a good system.

Smart

The devices we use have to do for us the things that we as humans have trouble doing—rapid computation, having infallible memories, detecting complicated patterns, and so forth. They need to remember the things we don't remember and do the work we can't easily do alone. They have to be smart.

Clever

Likewise, the best products predict the needs of their users and then fulfill those needs in unexpectedly pleasing ways. Adaptive targets are one way to do this with gestural interfaces. Another way to be clever is through interactive gestures that match well the action the user is trying to perform.

Playful

One area in which interactive gestures excel is being playful. Through play, users will not only start to engage with your interface—by trying it out to see how it works—but they will also explore new features and variations on their gestures. Users need to feel relaxed to engage in play. Errors need to be difficult to make so that there is no need to put warning messages all over the interface. The ability to undo mistakes is also crucial for fostering the environment for play. Play stops if users feel trapped, powerless, or lost.

---

* See *Field Guide to Gestures*, by Nancy Armstrong and Melissa Wagner (Quirk Books): 45–48.

Pleasurable

"Have nothing in your house," said William Morris, "that you do not know to be useful, or believe to be beautiful." Gestural interfaces should be both aesthetically and functionally pleasing. Humans are more forgiving of mistakes in beautiful things.* The parts of the gestural system—the visual interface; the input devices; the visual, aural, and haptic feedback—should be agreeable to the senses. They should be pleasurable to use. This engenders good feelings in their users.

Good

Gestural interfaces should have respect and compassion for those who will use them. It is very easy to remove human dignity with interactive gestures— for instance, by making people perform a gesture that makes them appear foolish in public, or by making it so difficult to perform a gesture that only the young and healthy can ever perform it. Designers and developers need to be responsible for the choices they make in their designs and ask themselves whether it is good for users, good for those indirectly affected, good for the culture, and good for the environment. The choices that are made with gestural interfaces need to be deliberate and forward-thinking. Every time users perform an interactive gesture, in an indirect way they are placing their trust in those who created it to have done their job ethically.

THE ATTRIBUTES OF GESTURES

Although touchscreen gestural interfaces differ slightly from free-form gestural interfaces, most gestures have similar characteristics that can be detected and thus designed for. The more sophisticated the interface (and the more sensors it employs), the more of these attributes can be engaged:

Presence

This is the most basic of all attributes. Something must be present to make a gesture in order to trigger an interaction. For some systems, especially in environments, a human being simply being present is enough to cause a reaction. For the simplest of touchscreens, the presence of a fingertip creates a touch event.

Duration

All gestures take place over time and can be done quickly or slowly. Is the user tapping a button or holding it down for a long period? Flicking the screen or sliding along it? For some interfaces, especially those that are simple, duration is less important. Interfaces using proximity sensors, for instance, care little for duration and only whether a human being is in the area. But for games and other types of interfaces, the ability to determine duration is crucial.

---

* See Don Norman's book, *Emotional Design* (Basic Books), for a detailed discussion of this topic.

Duration is measured by calculating the time of first impact or sensed movement compared to the end of the gesture.

Position

Where is the gesture being made? From a development standpoint, position is often determined by establishing an *x/y* location on an axis (such as the entire screen) and then calculating any changes. Some gestures also employ the *z*-axis of depth. Note that because of human beings' varying heights, position can be relational (related to the relative size of the person) or exact (adjusted to the parameters of the room). For instance, a designer may want to put some gestures high in an environment so that children cannot engage in them.

Motion

Is the user moving from position to position or striking a pose in one place? Is the motion fast or slow? Up and down, or side to side? For some systems, any motion is enough to trigger a response; position is unnecessary to determine.

Pressure

Is the user pressing hard or gently on a touchscreen or pressure-sensitive device? This too has a wide range of sensitivity. You may want every slight touch to register, or only the firmest, or only an adult weight (or only that of a child or pet). Note that some pressure can be "faked" by duration; the longer the press/movement, the more "pressure" it has. Pressure can also be faked by trying to detect an increasing spread of a finger pad: as we press down, the pad of our finger widens slightly as it presses against a surface.

Size

Width and height can also be combined to measure size. For example, touchscreens can determine whether a user is employing a stylus or a finger based on size (the tip of a stylus will be finer) and adjust themselves accordingly.

Orientation

What direction is the user (or the device) facing while the gesture is being made? For games and environments, this attribute is extremely important. Orientation has to be determined using fixed points (such as the angle of the user to the object itself).

Including objects

Some gestural interfaces allow users to employ physical objects alongside their bodies to enhance or engage the system. Simple systems will treat these other objects as an extension of the human body, but more sophisticated ones will recognize objects and allow users to employ them in context.

For instance, a system could see a piece of paper a user is holding as being simply part of the user's hand, whereas another system, such as the Digital Desk system (see Figure 1-12, earlier in this chapter), might see it as a piece of paper that can have text or images projected onto it.

Number of touch points/combination

More and more gestural interfaces have multitouch capability, allowing users to use more than one finger or hand simultaneously to control them. They may also allow combinations of gestures to occur at the same time. One common example is using two hands to enlarge an image by dragging on two opposite corners, seemingly stretching the image.

Figure 1-17. *Designers experimenting with a multitouch system to play Starcraft with two hands. Courtesy Harry van der Veen and Natural User Interface.*

Sequence

Interactive gestures don't necessarily have to be singular. A wave followed by a fist can trigger a different action than both of those gestures done separately. Of course, this means a very sophisticated system that remembers states. This is also more difficult for users (see "States and Modes," later in this chapter).

Ball and socket

A ball and socket joint, such as that of the hip and shoulder, consists of one rounded bone fitting into the cup-like depression of another. Ball and socket joints allow for a wide range of movement in a circular motion around the center of the "ball."

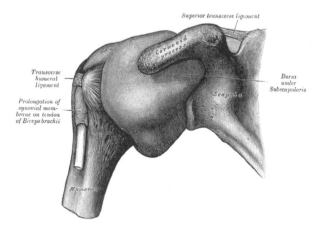

Figure 2-2. *The shoulder is a ball and socket joint. Courtesy Gray's Anatomy.*

Condyloid

A condyloid joint, such as the wrist, is similar to a ball and socket joint, except that the condyloid has no socket; the ball rests against the end of a bone instead.

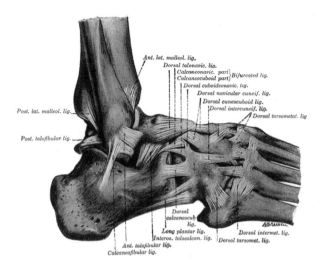

Figure 2-3. *The wrist and the ankle (shown) are examples of condyloid joints. Courtesy Gray's Anatomy.*

Gliding

Some of the bones in the wrists and ankles move (in a very limited way) by sliding against each other. These gliding joints occur where the surfaces of two flat bones are held together by ligaments.

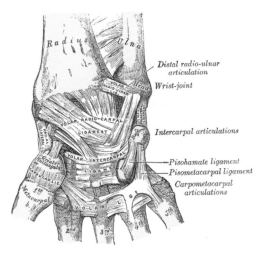

Figure 2-4. *The hand is filled with ligaments that allow for limited movement via gliding joints. Courtesy Gray's Anatomy.*

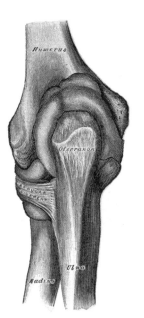

Hinge

A hinge joint, such as the elbow or those in the fingers, moves in only one plane, back and forth, acting like the hinge of a door (hence the name).

Pivot

The pivot joint in your neck allows you to turn your head from side to side. Pivot joints are limited in rotation and are made up of one bone fitting into a ring of bone and ligaments.

Figure 2-5. *The knee and elbow (shown) are examples of hinge joints. Courtesy Gray's Anatomy.*

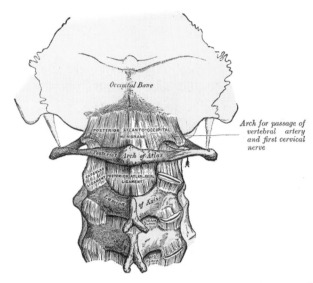

Figure 2-6. *The skull fits into the spinal column in a ring of bone and ligaments, forming a pivot joint that allows the head to turn. Courtesy Gray's Anatomy.*

Saddle

The only saddle joints in the human body are the thumbs. Saddle joints occur where one bone fits like a saddle on top of another. Saddle joints can rock back and forth and can rotate, much like the condyloid joints.

These joints are the fulcrums on which all the major movements of the body occur. The only other joints we should be concerned with are those between the vertebrae in the spine, connected by pads of cartilage, which can move slightly, allowing for bends and twists of the whole torso.

MOTIONS

The medical and kinesiology communities have technical terms for the types of movement the human body is capable of. Frequently, these movements come in pairs: first, there is the execution of the movement, and then the opposite movement that returns the body or limb to a neutral state. The human body is capable of the following broad movements:

Flexion and extension

A movement that decreases the angle between two parts of the body, such as making a fist or bending an elbow, is called a **flexion**. Applied to a ball and socket joint such as the hip or shoulder, *flexion* means the limb has moved forward. The opposite motion is an **extension**. Extensions increase the angle between two body parts and, in effect, straighten limbs. When you stand up, you cause your knees to extend. Extending the hip or shoulder moves the full limb (leg or arm) backward.

Rotation

Rotation is any movement in which a body part (aided by a ball and socket, condyloid, pivot, or saddle joint) turns on its axis. Twiddling your thumbs is an example of a rotation.

Abduction and adduction

Abduction is a motion that moves one part of the body away from its midline. The **midline** is an imaginary line that divides the body (or a limb) in left/right halves. When referring to fingers and toes, abduction means spreading the digits apart, away from the centerline of the hand or foot. Raising an arm up and to the side is an example of abduction. Adduction is a motion that moves a part of the body toward the body's midline or toward the midline of a limb. Putting splayed fingers back together is an example of adduction.

Internal and external rotation

Internal rotation turns a limb toward the body's midline. An internal rotation of the hip, for example, would point the toes inward. An external rotation would do the opposite: point the toes outward, away from the midline of the body.

Elevation and depression

Any movement upward, such as lifting a leg, is an elevation. Depression is the opposite.

Protraction and retraction

Protraction is the forward movement of an arm, and retraction is the backward stretching movement of the arm. Similarly, protrusion and retrusion are the forward (protrusion) and backward (retrusion) movements of a body part, frequently the jaw.

In addition to these major, broad movements, there are specialized movements that only the hands and feet can perform. These, too, often come in pairs:

Supination and pronation

Supination occurs when the forearm rotates and the palm of the hand turns upward. The opposite motion, which turns the palm down, is pronation.

Plantarflexion and dorsiflexion

Two types of flexion of the foot are plantarflexion and dorsiflexion. Plantarflexion is a flexion that pushes the foot down, as though pushing a gas pedal. Dorsiflexion is its opposite: a movement that moves the foot upward.

Eversion and inversion

Eversion moves the sole of the foot outward, in effect turning the foot sideways. Inversion, which can occur accidentally when the ankle is twisted, turns the sole inward.

a PPI of 85 is only 34 pixels, almost two-thirds smaller.* In short, whenever possible, measure and prototype your touch targets using actual dimensions and resolutions to ensure that they are correctly sized (see Chapter 6 for more on prototyping). Ideally, you will want to test the touch targets with users as well.

All that being said, many touchscreen devices on the market have much smaller touch targets than this guideline, particularly when it comes to on-screen keyboards.

Figure 2-9. *The keyboard on the iPhone contains some of the smallest touch targets (5 mm or 0.2 inches) of any gestural interface. It uses adaptive targets to partially get around this limitation. Courtesy Nick Richards.*

Figure 2-10. *An illustration of an iceberg tip. The dotted line represents the invisible edge of the touch target.*

There are two ways around the size limitations of touch targets: iceberg tips and adaptive targets. Like icebergs that are mostly underwater, **iceberg tips** are controls that have a larger target than what is visible. That is, the touch target is larger than the visible icon representing it. Using iceberg tips, designers can increase the size of the touch target without increasing the size of the object itself, which can lead to large, ungainly icons. The implications of this, however, are that there has to be enough space between objects to create this effect. Objects that are directly adjacent won't be able to use this trick to its best effect, unless they make use of adaptive targets.

---

* See *https://help.ubuntu.com/community/UMEGuide/DesigningForFingerUIs* for a table of some common screen sizes and the corresponding minimum button size.

Adaptive targets are created algorithmically by guessing the next item the user will touch, then increasing the touch target appropriately. Usually, this increases the hidden part of the "iceberg" as described earlier, not the object itself, although that too is possible. This trick is often used with keyboards, such as on the iPhone. For example, if a user types the letters *t* and *h* in a row, the system predicts that the next likely letter the user will type is *e* (forming the word *the*), and not the letters *r*, *w*, or *d* or the number *3* (i.e., the keys in the general area surrounding *e* that a user might accidentally touch). Of course, designers and developers need to be careful not to overpredict users' actions, and when making such predictions to always allow users to undo the guess, via either a Delete key or an undo command.

ACCESSIBILITY

Obviously, some gestural interfaces will be extremely difficult for those with physical challenges to operate, especially for those with limited hand movement. Although no guidelines exist yet, to be accessible to the widest possible user base, touch targets will have to be large (perhaps 150% of the typical size, or 1.5 cm square) and gestures simple and limited (taps, waves, proximity alone). Anything beyond some basic movements (tap, wave, flick, press) that use single fingers or the whole hand as one entity may be challenging for some disabled users. Even patterns such as *Pinch to Shrink* can be tricky.

On the positive side, some gestural interfaces might be more accessible than most keyboard/mouse systems, requiring only gross motor skills or facial recognition to engage them.

The body is an amazingly flexible tool with a wide variety of gestures. The hands alone have the potential for hundreds of possible configurations that could be used to trigger a system response. It is just up to designers to employ them correctly and not to overstrain users.

The next two chapters examine gestural interfaces that combine some of these physical gestures with system behaviors to form a pattern. Chapter 3 examines those patterns for direct manipulation, and Chapter 4 details those for indirect manipulation.

FOR FURTHER READING

Designing for People, Henry Dreyfuss (Allworth Press)

Abstracting Craft: The Practiced Digital Hand, Malcolm McCullough (MIT Press)

The Measure of Man and Woman: Human Factors in Design, Alvin R. Tilley and Henry Dreyfuss (Wiley)

Figure 3-5. *Subway's sandwich ordering kiosk has users select condiments. Courtesy Justin Hall.*

Figure 3-6. *This Twinkle application for the Apple iPhone allows users to select Twitter messages from a list. Courtesy Nick Starr.*

DRAG TO MOVE OBJECT

WHAT

Using a single finger on top of an object on-screen moves that object, along with the finger, to a new location.

USE WHEN

Use this pattern for drag-and-drop, sliders, and other controls to enable the user to move an object to another part of the screen.

WHY

Without being able to grasp and pick up an object, users still need a way to move objects, so pushing and pulling them with their finger is a natural action to accomplish this. Some controls, such as sliders, require this pattern.

HOW

Either the object has to be selected first, or this gesture has to be combined with *Tap to Select* so that an object that is beneath a touch event can be automatically selected and moved with the finger as it moves across the screen. Objects on-screen can be constrained to slide in only certain directions (e.g., left and right on a slider).

EXAMPLES

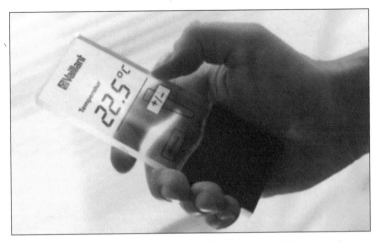

Figure 3-7. *A concept for Comfort, an environmental system controlled by a touchscreen remote control. Sliding a thumb down the slider changes the temperature. Courtesy Valliant.*

Figure 3-8. *The iPhone's Slide to Unlock feature lets users slide the "latch" in only one direction, which is indicated with both an arrow and an animation on the words "slide to unlock." Courtesy John Pastor.*

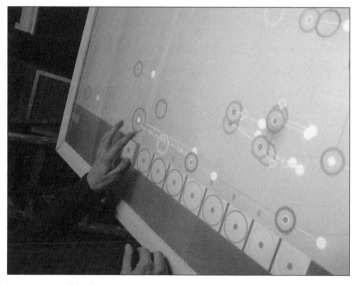

Figure 3-9. *You control the loopArenaMTC music device by sliding musical "agents" with your fingertip. You activate the agents by touching and moving them into different positions. Courtesy Jens Wunderling.*

SLIDE TO SCROLL

WHAT

This is similar to *Drag to Move Object*, but in this pattern, sliding a finger on the screen in one direction scrolls the screen or a list of items in that direction. You can use this along with *Slide and Hold for Continuous Scroll*.

USE WHEN

Use *Slide to Scroll* when content that users want to access resides outside the visible viewing area, such as text drifting off the screen, a large map, or a large data set such as search results. You can also use this for moving through simple menus.

WHY

Many screens, especially on mobile devices, have a limited area in which to view content, so scrolling is necessary. *Slide to Scroll*, along with *Fling to Scroll*, is a simple way to accomplish this scrolling. It is also used extensively on trackpads.

HOW

The system should check to make sure the user isn't performing *Drag to Move Object* by seeing whether the finger and an object align, and if they don't, by then moving the screen in the direction of the slide if possible. (If that is not possible, some sort of feedback, such as a bounce or sound, should trigger.) For clarity, you should not use this pattern with *Two Fingers to Scroll*.

Scroll bars indicating position can also be helpful, either always visible or appearing as necessary.

Utilizing some kind of feedback, such as a visual bounce, haptic buzz, or sound when the user reaches the end of a scroll, is a good practice.

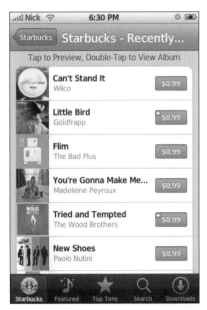

Figure 3-26. *The Starbucks version of iTunes on the iPhone allows users to scroll through a list of songs recently played in the store. Tapping the scrolling list stops it. Courtesy Nick Starr.*

Figure 3-27. *The Zune allows you to stop scrolling lists with a tap. Courtesy Microsoft.*

PINCH TO SHRINK AND SPREAD TO ENLARGE

WHAT

Two fingers—either the thumb and index finger on a single hand, or both left and right index fingers if both hands are used—are brought closer together (*Pinch to Shrink*) or farther apart (*Spread to Enlarge*) while on top of an object, causing that object to change in size, scaling smaller if the fingers are moving closer together and larger if the fingers move farther apart. These two patterns are almost always found together.

USE WHEN

Use these patterns to increase or decrease the size of objects (e.g., maps, web pages, documents, images) or the entire screen, effectively zooming in and out.

WHY

For small devices in particular, users may need to zoom in and zoom out to see an object at the correct level of fidelity and detail. This also effectively eliminates a need to increase font size for some objects with text.

HOW

These two patterns require a system to be able to recognize two touch events (multitouch). The patterns typically scale an object proportionally, although it doesn't necessarily have to be so. They also typically utilize a smooth motion on a scale, not set levels of shrinking. That is, the starting points of the two fingers are usually equal to 100% of the object's starting size. As the fingers move closer together or farther apart, the object scales in real time to match the new distance between the fingers at a ratio that designers will need to determine based on the sizes of the original objects and the size of the screen. For instance, if the fingers are 50% closer, the object could be 50% of its original size, or it could be another percentage altogether. There can be, however, a point beyond which a user cannot (or should not) shrink or enlarge an object (thus making it impossible to see or interact with), and that point should be predetermined.

Figure 4-2. *Swinxs is an outdoor game console for children. Several of the games, such as the racing and hide-and-seek games, involve getting close to the base station with the (included) wristband. For example, in the case of a racing game, Swinxs would use the wearer's proximity to the base station to determine the winner. Courtesy Swinxs BV.*

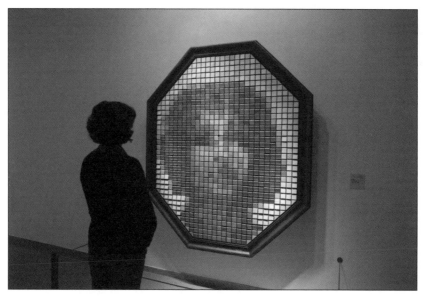

Figure 4-3. *The Wooden Mirror, which comprises a camera and dozens of individual slats of wood on motors, "reflects" the image of the person standing in front of it. Courtesy Danny Rozen.*

MOVE BODY TO ACTIVATE

WHAT

The physical movement of the body or a part of the body (not just its presence as in *Proximity Activates/Deactivates* and not a specific gesture) triggers an action.

USE WHEN

Use this when the action you are enabling requires that the person be moving, not just be in an area (as in *Proximity Activates/Deactivates*). This pattern is often found in alarms and other environmental systems.

WHY

Instead of *Proximity Activates/Deactivates*, use *Move Body to Activate* either because the movement itself is meaningful (e.g., an activity such as dancing or running) and the action triggered is related to that motion, or to prevent false triggering.

HOW

This pattern requires the ability to sense movement—frequently, directional movement. This can be accomplished with cameras or infrared beams, or via accelerometers embedded in wearable devices.

EXAMPLES

Figure 4-4. The Nike+iPod Sports Kit consists of an accelerometer that is attached to or embedded in a shoe, which communicates to an iPod Nano. Users can track in real time their calories burned, distance, or time while running. Courtesy Apple.

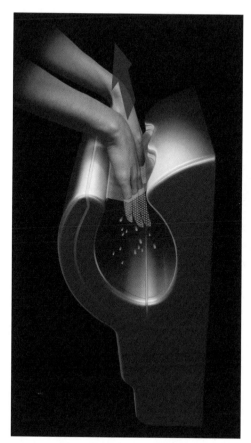

Figure 4-14. *The unfortunately named Dyson AirBlade (it doesn't sound like something I'd want to stick my hands into) dries wet hands that are placed into and slowly drawn out of the device. Courtesy Dyson.*

Figure 4-15. *The Sensor Soap Pump uses an infrared sensor to detect when hands are placed beneath its spout. Courtesy simplehuman.*

ROTATE TO CHANGE STATE

WHAT

Turning or tilting an object changes either the functionality of the object or the feedback/display of items on that object.

USE WHEN

Use *Rotate to Change State* on devices that can be used for multiple purposes or to display content that might be better viewed in portrait or landscape view.

WHY

Particularly useful on devices with limited, rectangular screen real estate, *Rotate to Change State* allows content to be viewed in ways that best display the content, given the screen size.

HOW

Rotate to Change State requires a gyroscope or a multiaxis accelerometer to determine the position of the device. The threshold for the change in state (e.g., 90 degrees, 180 degrees, etc.) needs to be determined.

If the device lays flat (e.g., on a table), accelerometers may not pick up the rotation.

EXAMPLES

Figure 4-16. *Nokia's newer N series phones, such as the N95 (pictured), are equipped with accelerometers and can change views from portrait to landscape based on how they are held. Courtesy Nokia.*

Figure 4-17. *The "Bar of Soap" changes its functionality (from camera to PDA to phone to gaming device) based on how it is held, switching modes when rotated. Courtesy Brandon Thomas Taylor and MIT Media Lab.*

Figure 4-18. *Canon's PowerShot SD1000 changes its display (to portrait or landscape) based on how the user is holding it. Courtesy Canon.*

STEP TO ACTIVATE

WHAT

A user steps (either deliberately or unknowingly) onto a designated spot that triggers an action.

USE WHEN

Use *Step to Activate* when other proximity detectors (sound, infrared cameras, etc.) would be impractical, or for actions that would naturally be delivered by the feet (stepping, dancing, etc.).

WHY

This pattern is useful for alternative controls when the hands are occupied or for controls in low places where it would be difficult to reach with the hands.

HOW

Step to Activate typically requires a pressure sensor placed inside or beneath a flat object, sometimes to protect the sensor from hard stomps or presses.

EXAMPLES

Figure 4-19. *One of the many incarnations of Dance Dance Revolution, where players follow on-screen cues to step in various directions quickly to play the game (and thus to dance). Courtesy Warren Rohner.*

GEEKY STUFF YOU MIGHT CARE ABOUT

Laban's Theory of Effort

Rudolf Laban also devised a model for thinking about effort when performing a movement. By *effort*, he really means *dynamic* or *character*, which can be useful to think about for more advanced gestural interfaces when the character of the gesture is important (e.g., in playing games, making music, or creating visual art).

Laban observed that similar muscle movements could have widely different characteristics. For instance, punching someone in the face and lightly touching him on the cheek are almost the same movement, but the dynamics of the movement are very different. Laban noted that movements could be characterized along four continuums:

- Space: Motions can be direct or indirect; that is, a limb or digit can touch something or not.
- Weight: Motions can be strong or light. Strong motions are those that engage a lot of force. Slamming a fist onto a table instead of tapping it with a finger is one example.
- Time: A motion can be sudden or sustained.
- Flow: A motion can be bound or free; that is, a motion can be self-contained or part of an ongoing movement.

When considering a gesture to engage a particular feature, it could be useful to consider its effort to see whether it matches the character of the feature. For instance, a sustained gesture (a slow wave) to trigger a sudden action (turning on the lights) may not make sense.

BENESH MOVEMENT NOTATION

The Benesh System is another form of movement notation most frequently used for documenting choreography, particularly traditional ballet. Created by Rudolf Benesh and Joan Benesh in the late 1940s and published in 1956, the Benesh System has many similarities with Labanotation in that it uses abstract symbols on a staff to mark movement through time that can be synchronized with music. Unlike Labanotation, the staff has five lines and is read from left to right. The top of the staff indicates the top of the head, and the bottom line indicates the floor, with shoulders, waist, and knees in between.

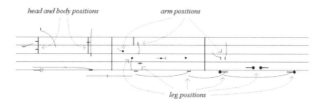

Figure 5-4. *An example of Benesh movement notation. Courtesy The Benesh Institute.*

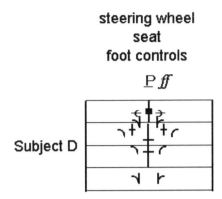

Figure 5-5. *Benesh notation of someone driving a car. The arms are flexed at the elbows and the hands are gripping each side of the steering wheel very tightly, with the wrists flexed. Courtesy The Benesh Institute.*

ESHKOL WACHMAN MOVEMENT NOTATION

Eshkol Wachman Movement Notation (EWMN) was created in 1958 by Noa Eshkol and Avraham Wachman. Although it is most frequently used for dance, it has also been applied to physical therapy, animal behavior, and even early diagnosis of autism. Unlike Labanotation and Benesh notation, EWMN doesn't take into account style or context (musical or otherwise).

EWMN uses a stick-figure skeleton (human or animal) as its conceptual starting point. EWMN looks at the body as a series of "limbs" that are bound by joints. For example, the forearm is a limb, with the wrist and elbow joints defining its endpoints, as is the foot between the ankle and the end of the toe. In EWMN terminology, limbs can be **heavy**. Heavy limbs are those that, when moved, force the lighter limbs attached to them to move involuntarily as well. Thus, moving the upper arm will also move the (relatively light) lower arm and the (even lighter) hand. Heavy limbs are relative, however. A typically light limb such as the hand can become a heavy limb if a handstand is being performed, for instance.

EWMN uses a three-dimensional sphere to plot the movements of the figure in space. Positions on the sphere can be mapped out with coordinates, similar to how positions on the globe can be indicated by longitude and latitude.

Steps

List in order the discreet moments in this piece of functionality.

Alternatives

List other use cases that may consider the same or similar functionality.

Related or alternative use cases

List other use cases that are similar to or that reference this use case.

Use cases, although time-consuming and, frankly, boring, are an excellent tool for breaking down tasks and showing what the system will have to support. They do, however, suffer the same sort of issues as do scenarios, task flows, and wireframes (discussed shortly)—namely, the difficulty of explaining human gestures in words.

For gestural interfaces, the most important parts of a use case are the initial and terminal conditions. Developers will make good use of those when determining the pattern for identifying when a gesture has begun and when it has ended.

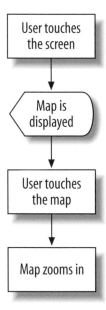

Figure 5-8. *Gestures should be represented in a task flow as a rectangle, with the top irregularly sloping up from left to right, indicating manual input.*

TASK ANALYSIS AND FLOWS

A **task analysis** is a list of activities that the product will have to support. Tasks can be drawn from the scenarios and use cases, as well as from requirements documentation and user research.

Once there is a task analysis, it is often helpful to put those tasks into a certain order, or **task flow**. Task flows are typically flowcharts that illustrate the activities and decisions throughout a process.

Task flows for gestural interfaces need to show decision points and the resultant actions for both the user and the system. The logic of the system (e.g., if a user makes *X* gesture, then *Y* happens; otherwise, *Z* happens) can determine not only the types and kinds of sensors required, but also the number of different gestures needed to "power" the system.

Initially, a task flow might contain generic actions ("User makes a gesture") until that gesture is determined and more richly documented via a wireframe, storyboard, animation, or movie.

WIREFRAMES

Wireframes are a form of paper prototype (see Chapter 6 for more on prototypes) that frequently strip down the visual and industrial design to a bare minimum so that viewers can focus their attention on the raw features, functionality, and content of a product. They explain the structure of a product in the same way that blueprints explain the structure of a building.

When they are for touchscreen systems, they are also often what designers call "pixel-perfect," meaning that the size of the objects on the wireframe matches to the pixel what will be seen on-screen. This is a good practice for touchscreens, as it prevents designers from overcrowding the screen and not leaving enough screen real estate for adequate touch targets.

Wireframes for gestural systems need to show:

Controls

What can be manipulated and how? What happens when a user touches the screen or an object, waves a hand, points, and so forth? Where are the controls placed? Unlike web design or even software design, the placement of controls for size, ergonomics, and to prevent screen coverage (see Chapter 1) needs to be specifically mapped out in wireframes.

Conditional objects and states

Wireframes need to define objects that change based on context. If a button cannot be tapped until an item is selected, that needs to be shown and explained. Ideally, every state that an object can be in (e.g., idle, selected, while dragged, while dropped, idle again) and the gesture that triggers that change in state should be shown.

Constraints

This means anything with a business, legal, technical, or physical constraint that prevents an action—especially if that action seems like it would be logical to perform, but cannot be performed. Sensor constraints are important to note (e.g., "The heat sensor only detects people within 5 meters").

Sensor settings

For free-form systems and even some projected interactive surfaces, it is important to note the setup of the sensors: their range, sphere of detection, and sensitivity. This may be difficult to determine on paper, as sensors can give a wide range of readings that can be accurately determined only via prototyping.

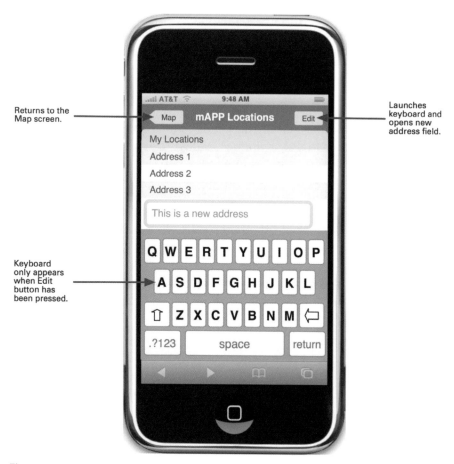

Figure 5-9. *An example of a pixel-perfect wireframe for a (fake) iPhone application, built using OmniGraffle stencils created by Theresa Neil.*

Describing how a product that makes use of interactive gestures works obviously requires showing how gestures engage the system. There are two ways to do this with wireframes: annotations and keyframes.

ANNOTATIONS

Annotations are the notes that explain pieces of functionality or controls that aren't obvious. For instance, an annotation might describe what happens when a user pushes a button or turns a dial.

> 👍 Use annotations to describe interactive gestures that are easy to understand, are in common use, and trigger a simple action.

There is likely no need, for instance, to document anything more complicated than noting "When the user taps this button with a finger, the device turns off." It's a simple, known gesture with a basic outcome. Any additional documentation is really overkill.

KEYFRAMES

When the interactive gesture (or the triggered system behavior) is slightly more complicated, designers can use keyframes to describe them. **Keyframes** are a concept appropriated from classic animation, when a senior animator would draw the important moments (key frames) in a story, leaving the junior animators to "fill in" the frames in between. For instance, the senior animator would draw the anvil falling from the sky and the coyote being crushed—enough to see the major incident—but other animators would draw the in-between frames later.

Figure 5-10. *An example of a simple, single-frame keyframe, showing how this tablet device with small touchpads can be locked. Courtesy David Fisher and Plastic Logic.*

At the low end, gestural movies can be a simple, single-shot, multisecond capture done with a hand-held video camera. At the high end, they can be complete stories with multiple shots using motion capture technology. **Motion capture** is the digital recording of an actor's movements via sensors (usually attached to the actor's body). In a motion capture session, the actor's movements (not her visual appearance) are sampled many times per second and recorded as animation data. A computer artist then overlays that data onto a digital 3D model, causing the model to move in the same manner. The artist can then manipulate the model using computer animation software.

Motion capture is obviously going to be out of the range of all but the most sophisticated (and well-funded!) companies. Rapid, guerilla-style filmmaking with a small digital camera is much more likely, and can be accomplished in a matter of minutes if necessary. After the motion is shot, simple movie-editing software such as Apple's iMovie or Microsoft's Windows Movie Maker can be used to edit, annotate, and export the video into something suitable for documentation.

INTEGRATING NONTRADITIONAL DOCUMENTATION

Once you have an animation or movie, the next challenge is to incorporate it into the world of traditional paper documentation since, let's face it, paper documentation is likely not going away anytime soon. The easiest way to ensure that movies and animations are used is, perhaps, to establish a website where they can be stored, viewed, and downloaded alongside other documentation. Paper documentation should contain links back to the site and, if possible, the animation or movie attached to emails sent with supporting documentation (or with documentation they support).

No matter which method or methods you choose to document your designs, it is important that the documentation allows the design to be prototyped and ultimately built. After all, as technologist David Verba pointed out,[*] few people get excited about a product from a wireframe. For that, you need a prototype, and that is the subject of the next chapter.

---

[*] See his presentation, "Sketching in Code," at *http://uxweek2007.adaptivepath.com/slides/uxweek-slides_verba_sketching_in_code.pdf*.

FOR FURTHER READING

Communicating Design: Developing Web Site Documentation for Design and Planning, Dan Brown (New Riders Press)

Sketching User Experiences: Getting the Design Right and the Right Design, Bill Buxton (Morgan Kaufmann)

Choreographics: A Comparison of Dance Notation Systems from the Fifteenth Century to the Present, Anne Hutchinson Guest (Routledge)

Understanding Comics: The Invisible Art, Scott McCloud (Harper Paperbacks)

Physical Computing—Representations of Human Movement in Human-Computer Interaction, Astrid Twenebowa Larssen (Springer Berlin)

When designing free-form interactive gestures for an environmental system, the options for low-fidelity prototyping are limited. About the best you can do is combine some rough physical models (if necessary to create the locations of sensors and the objects the gestural system can control) with manual control of the objects in the environment—in other words, having a "man behind the curtain" (discussed shortly). Remote controls, other devices such as mobile phones, and even fishing wire can be used to manually control objects (or prototypes of objects).

Figure 6-5. Crescendo Design uses Second Life to model physical spaces as part of its professional practice, to describe design ideas to long-distance clients. Courtesy Jon Brouchoud, Crescendo Design.

One alternative that some designers and architects are exploring to physically prototype spaces is to model environments in a virtual world, such as Second Life.* The cost in materials and physical space is obviously nil, and objects and interactions can be easily created and tweaked right in the virtual environment (or in other 3D software). One drawback is that gestures created by avatars can be primitive, and they certainly don't have the full range of motion of the human body, especially the hands; nor do virtual spaces provide the immersive testing environment that can bring an interactive system to life. Nevertheless, they can be a viable alternative for creating a rough model of an environment.

---

* For more information, see The Arch, a blog by Jon Brouchoud at *http://archsl.wordpress.com/*.

"THE MAN BEHIND THE CURTAIN"

Since low-fidelity prototypes are, by nature, quickly put together and may be only somewhat interactive (if at all), they often require that someone control them to make them appear interactive. This someone—the "man behind the curtain" (named for the famous scene in the movie *The Wizard of Oz*: "Pay no attention to that man behind the curtain!")—can be hidden from sight or be out in the open, depending on how realistic the designers want the experience to be. (This technique is sometimes called the Wizard of Oz technique.)

> ✍ Employ a "man behind the curtain" to manipulate a low-fidelity prototype into seeming more interactive than it really is.

Obviously, with paper prototypes or rough physical models, no type of functionality can be controlled remotely; it all has to be done manually and in sight. But with a digital prototype, the "man behind the curtain" can literally be behind a curtain (or a one-way mirror), controlling a device that only seems interactive from another (hidden) location. As a user makes a gesture, the man behind the curtain triggers the system to respond as it normally would if the correct sensors, mechanics, and so on were in place. *Voilà!* An interactive, gestural system.

Man-behind-the-curtain functionality can save quite a bit of the time, effort, and money that it takes to prototype a working system, and it can also provide valuable feedback if you do decide to build a high-fidelity prototype.

Figure 6-6. *This test of a touchscreen navigation system for a robot had subjects using a prototype of the touchscreen on a laptop while the designers followed behind, controlling the system via a wireless keyboard as the subjects touched the screen. Courtesy Jeff Howard and Andrew Ko.*

HIGH-FIDELITY PROTOTYPES

Low-fidelity prototypes can tell you only so much. Once the general concepts, gestures, and flows have been prototyped with low-fidelity methods, it is time to focus on making a prototype that closely mimics the actual experience of the final product: a high-fidelity prototype. If low-fidelity prototypes are about testing concepts, high-fidelity prototypes are about refining those concepts, making sure that what looks good on paper still looks good once it is "alive." The difference between high- and low-fidelity prototypes is simply this: the high-fidelity prototype (mostly) works as it should. When a gesture is made, something happens that doesn't require a "man behind the curtain" or a designer to explain it. The system behaves as it would in the field.

👍 Use high-fidelity prototypes to test and refine the details of the gestural system.

Figure 6-7. With a high-fidelity prototype, you are able to test such things as legibility and ergonomics. Courtesy Stimulant.

As the name suggests, these prototypes require a more serious investment in time and resources to create. With high-fidelity prototypes, the idea is to design and test as many of the details as possible—in interaction, environmental, industrial, and visual design, as well as in engineering and code. Even though it occurs only occasionally, designers, developers, and engineers should strive to create high-fidelity prototypes that are nearly indistinguishable from the product a user would buy or encounter. The less the high-fidelity prototype seems like a prototype, the more accurate the feedback will be about the experience of using it. Users won't be thrown by, say, being handed a lump of wires, a sensor, and a battery and being told to imagine they are holding a kitchen appliance. With a high-fidelity prototype, the aesthetics matter.

Plumbing, however, does not matter. Prototypes should not be production- or manufacturing-ready (that would make them the actual products, not prototypes). They have to work just enough to, well, work. Prototypes, even high-fidelity ones, should be built to be thrown away eventually. Assuming that you can reuse code or engineering from a prototype leads to delays in prototype development and possibly even a lower-quality final product.

THE THREE TYPES OF HIGH-FIDELITY PROTOTYPES

There are three types of high-fidelity prototypes, categorized by what it takes to build them: exact, off-the-shelf, and do-it-yourself. With an **exact prototype**, you have as the prototyping environment the exact device on which the software will run. This is obviously the best-case scenario, as you'll get the most accurate results with it and usually the hard work of constructing the device has already been done for you.

But when that device is unavailable or doesn't exist yet, you need to create it. **Off-the-shelf (OTS) prototypes** make use of existing hardware and software to build the prototype, whereas **do-it-yourself (DIY) prototypes** are handcrafted and require much more assembly and general know-how to manufacture. If you need a soldering iron to make it, it is definitely a DIY prototype. Most prototypes for touchscreens are now exact or OTS prototypes, whereas prototypes of free-form interactive gestures are mostly DIY prototypes.

EXACT PROTOTYPES

Exact prototypes are for when you are designing for an existing platform or known piece of hardware. If you are designing for an iPhone, Wii, Nokia late-model N series device, IBM touchscreen kiosk, and so forth, there is no reason not to use the existing and readily available hardware for a high-fidelity prototype. What you need to do is to acquire the necessary drivers, manuals, or APIs to put your code onto the device (and to know what programming languages it supports in the first place).

Even though it is easier than creating a device from scratch, creating an exact prototype can still be quite difficult and time-consuming because you are forced to develop for a specific environment—one with which you may not be very familiar. You may even have to partner with an outside developer who has a particular expertise if you or your team doesn't know the necessary language. For example, mobile devices require specialized expertise in programming frameworks such as J2ME, .NET Mobile, S60, and the iPhone SDK.

All device manufacturers help developers and designers by providing documentation. In addition to basic documentation, some companies provide **software development kits (SDKs)**. An SDK is a set of software tools and possibly hardware that facilitate the creation of applications for a device. You will find

Communicating Interactive Gestures

" The perception of what a thing is and the perception of what it means are not separate, either. "

—James Gibson

When Antenna Design set out to redesign New York City's Metropolitan Transit Authority's (MTA) ticket vending machines,* it initially assumed that everyone would realize the machines had touchscreens. After all, they figured, everyone had used ATMs and touchscreen kiosks at airports. But they found that, because the MTA serves literally tens of millions of people from all walks of life, a large percentage of its users had never done those things. They didn't know what it was like to use an ATM because they didn't even have a bank account.

Thus, when it came time to design the screen for the MetroCard Vending Machines, Antenna Design needed to provide an extremely obvious visual cue that the kiosk was a touchscreen.

Figure 7-1. *Even though you can touch anywhere on the screen to begin, Antenna Design wanted to make sure the instructions were dead simple, with two written cues and an animated hand to remove all ambiguity, even for tourists who do not read English. Courtesy Antenna Design.*

---

* As related by Antenna Design partner, Sigi Moeslinger, at Interaction08. Watch the video at *http://interaction08. ixda.org/Sigi_Moeslinger.php.*

Especially with free-form interactive gestures but also with touchscreens, it increasingly isn't enough to simply install a product and hope for the best. As noted in Chapter 1, the best gestural interfaces need to be *discoverable*. Users need to be made aware of their presence and, after that, their affordances. What can I do here? How can I activate and engage with this? What are the controls?

Designer Clive Grinyer relates a humorous anecdote* that brings the need for communication into stark relief:

> I work in Paris, in a large converted telephone exchange where we have recently installed new light switches that save energy by turning off when they don't detect movement. When you go to the loo, you don't move much, you might move bits of you, or you might grimace a bit, but it's not movement as such, certainly not detectable by the infrared monitor. So, after 20 seconds, the light goes off.

> Someone, somewhere, made the decision that after 20 seconds the light would go off. It might have been the facilities manager. It was more likely the person who set the default, probably the kind-hearted engineer who programmed these switches. He (and it was almost certainly a He) went home feeling good. He may have even told his kids that he had saved the world a few kilowatts, that he was doing his bit against George Bush (especially if he was French), and felt happy and satisfied when he went to sleep that night.

> But the experience I am having of his decision is that I am sitting on a loo in a foreign country waving my arms about because I think there is probably a sensor somewhere, if only I could see it, which will eventually see me and turn the light back on.

Although clearly this is an example of bad design (20 seconds is an awfully short period of time), this story amply indicates that communicating interactive gestures means communicating two pieces of information:

Presence
> Alert potential users that a gestural system is available to them.

Instruction
> Teach users how to engage with the system. This includes the most basic instruction, namely, how do I turn this thing on (or off)?

These two things can be delivered in a variety of ways over a variety of distances from the product.

---

* Read the whole post, "Technology doesn't work," at *http://blog.clivegrinyer.com/blog/_archives/2007/2/13/2733052. html*.

THREE ZONES OF ENGAGEMENT

Most gestural interfaces have three zones of engagement,* which happen in space relative to the size of the device:

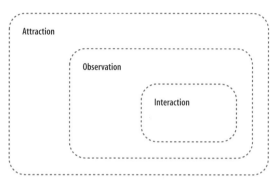

Figure 7-2. The three zones of engagement. The nearer to the product the user is, the more variety of communication methods can be employed to engage the user.

Figure 7-3. This touchscreen kiosk for HP's Photosmart Express is wrapped in signage to attract users in locations such as supermarkets and pharmacies. Note how the signs peek above the height of the shelves, and there is even a mat on the aisle floor. Courtesy Hewlett-Packard.

Attraction

A person spots the product or output from the product, such as a sound, and is (hopefully) interested and intrigued by it. This typically happens from a distance—for large environmental displays, this could be from very far away. Often the attraction is triggered by environmental cues such as signage, sound, or the hardware of the product itself, or it could simply be that the person notices someone using the system. The gestures themselves, if broad enough, could also be enough to attract attention.

---

* This framework was suggested by Darren David and Nathan Moody of Stimulant.

Observation

From midrange, a person is able to see more detail about the product and the gestures involved in engaging with it. At this point, environmental cues such as signage are crucial. Signage can both instruct and engage at this distance. It's also from this distance that users can demonstrate to others how a product works. Observers learn the UI conventions of the product just by watching and asking questions.

Figure 7-4. *From other parts of the room, one can watch others playing with the Wii and thus learn how to play the game. Courtesy Dru Kelly.*

Figure 7-5. *Samsung's Anycall Haptic mobile phone's controls (such as those for all small, personal devices) are meant to be viewed and controlled only by someone holding the device. Courtesy Samsung.*

Interaction

From up close (within a meter/yard of most devices), the person can become a user, directly interacting with the product. The instructions and affordances here are likely on the product itself, meant to be seen and read from very nearby.

When designing a gestural system, it is good to keep these three zones in mind so that proper communication channels can be established and designed early, and the correct communication methods (discussed shortly) are used.

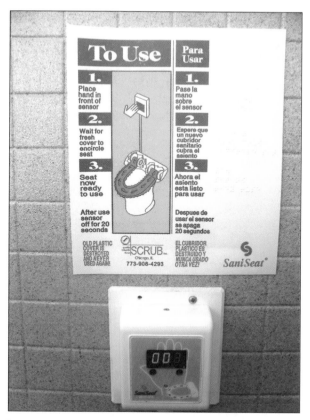

Figure 7-10. *This SaniSeat shows where the hand is placed, but the rest of the system is so compli-cated (at least for a public toilet) that it requires a poster to explain.*

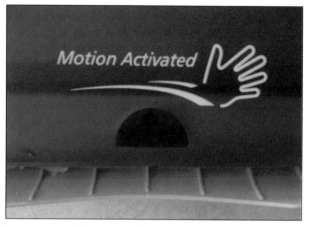

Figure 7-11. *This paper towel dispenser combines a well-designed illustration showing the left-to-right movement required to trigger the device, with a small bit of text to show presence.*

Figure 7-12. *Apparently, public restrooms are excellent places to find gestural interfaces.*

We've been discussing the communication of gestures, mostly in real time, in the context in which they are being performed. However, you can also apply all of these techniques in user manuals, help files, marketing brochures, and packaging—places where the communication doesn't always occur while the gesture is taking place, but rather before or after.

Zoom in or out
- Pinch to zoom in or out.

Figure 7-13. *Although the best instruction is contextual, manuals can sometimes enlighten with more detail than would be delivered on-screen or in an environment. From the iPod Touch Features Manual. Courtesy Apple, Inc.*

DEMONSTRATION

A demonstration is a moving image that shows the gesture that needs to be performed. This can be a simple, animated illustration or it can be a live-action movie with an actor performing the gesture. Of course, this necessitates some sort of display that can show motion: either a device monitor or TV screen, or a projector projecting the imagery onto a surface. (In theory, a 2D holograph could obviate the need for a monitor in certain situations where a screen would be impractical or impossible.)

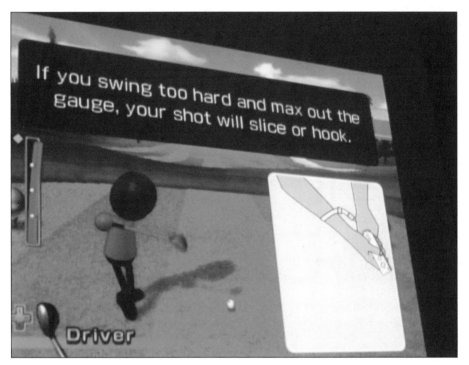

Figure 7-14. During game play, Wii games occasionally pop up demonstrations to help players learn or refine their gestures. Watching while doing is a powerful way to learn a gesture. Courtesy JasonJT.

Demonstrations typically show an animated movement in a loop so that it can be imitated to initiate an action. The animated hand touching the MTA vending machine discussed at the beginning of this chapter is an example of a simple demonstration.

USE OF SYMBOLS

There has been some activity, particularly in the ubiquitous computing community, to create symbols that indicate when an interactive system is present in a space when it would otherwise be invisible. Like other methods, these symbols can communicate presence and instruct users on how to use the system.

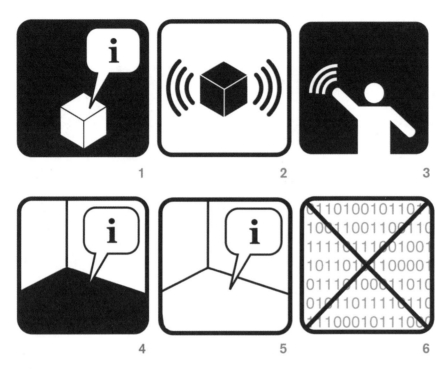

Figure 7-15. A sample from a set of ubiquitous computing icons from Adam Greenfield and Nurri Kim. 1: This object is self-describing. 2: This object has imperceptible qualities. 3: A gestural interface is available. 4: This location is self-describing. 5: A variation on #4. 6: Network dead zone; no information collected in this area.

Figure 7-16. Part of an icon set originally conceived for use with RFID technology and inspired by existing icons for push buttons, contact cards, and instructional diagrams. Courtesy Timo Arnall.

These symbols, however, are not in common use, and until they are, it is unwise to assume that simply putting one of these symbols on a sign will be enough to communicate to most users—at least in the short term. In the future, however, one can easily see that a universal set of symbols could be an extremely useful and powerful tool for designers.

SIMILE AND METAPHOR

It can be beneficial, both when designing and particularly when communicating designs, to think in terms of simile and metaphor. Metaphor for gestural interfaces makes perfect sense, as you are trying to turn something abstract (a digital system that is likely mostly invisible) into something concrete, controlled by the body. Metaphors, which turn abstract concepts into the concrete ("Time is money"), are the perfect tool for this.

You can say, "Make your hand flat and hold it up and move it back and forth, left and right," but it is much easier to say, "Wave." This is true not only for simple gestures but also for complex ones, perhaps even more so. "Move your hand like you are stirring a pot" is considerably easier to describe than it would be otherwise.

However, as noted in Chapters 1 and 2, gestures on their own do contain meaning, and that meaning can become mixed up with another metaphor that you try to lay on top of it. For instance, if your "stirring the pot" gesture has nothing to do with mixing something (e.g., images, sounds, etc.), users may be confused by it, and certainly might have difficulty remembering it.

👍 The best metaphors are those that match the understood meaning of the gesture with the action being performed.

We should never forget that the products we design do live in the world, often in specific contexts. How we create messages about a product in that context is essential to the life cycle of the product, but it also changes the environment, for good or ill. A beautiful gestural interface can quickly be ruined or tainted by the signage and hardware around it. The communication of a product's presence and use also communicates, directly or indirectly, its value and meaning.

FOR FURTHER READING

Everyware: The Dawning Age of Ubiquitous Computing, Adam Greenfield (New Riders Publishing)

Universal Principles of Design, William Lidwell, Kritina Holden, and Jill Butler (Rockport Publishers)

The Elements of Style, William Strunk and E.B. White (Coyote Canyon Press)

Metaphors We Live By, George Lakoff and Mark Johnson (University of Chicago Press)

The Future of Interactive Gestures

" Tomorrow will give us something to think about. "

—Cicero

Predicting the future is a sucker's game. But there is far more to interactive gestures than check-in kiosks, towel dispensers, and the nearly ubiquitous demonstration of scaling and sorting photos! As prices decrease and the availability of these devices (and the tools to create them) increases, we will see more novel implementations of touchscreens everywhere.

Of course, this may not be an entirely good thing. As Chapter 1 pointed out, gestural interfaces shouldn't be used for everything: they are a poor choice, for instance, for heavy data input. But assuredly, we'll see them being used for activities for which they weren't meant to be used, as well as for applications for which we never expected to use them. Despite the long history of this technology, we're entering a time—an interesting and exciting time—much like the early days of the Web in the 1990s or the beginning of personal computing in the 1970s and 1980s, when experimentation and exploration are the norms, when we're still figuring out standards and best practices and what this technology can really do.

FUTURE TRENDS

It took about six years for the gestural system in *Minority Report* to move from science fiction to reality; what will the next six years bring? Here are my predictions.

WIDESPREAD ADOPTION IN THE HOME AND OFFICE

We've seen gestural interfaces in public spaces such as public restrooms, retail environments, and airports. But touchscreens haven't entirely penetrated the home and office environment as of yet (at least not until, like any mature technology, they become invisible and "natural"). But that is changing quickly. Consumer electronics manufacturers are rapidly producing new lines of products that employ touchscreens. As *BusinessWeek* reported,* companies around the world are designing and producing new products with gestural interfaces:

> " *The touch-screen tech ecosystem now includes more than 100 companies specializing in everything from smudge-proof screens to sensors capable of detecting fingers before they even contact the screen. Sales of leading touch-screen technologies, such as those used in mobile phones and navigation devices, are expected to rise to $4.4 billion in 2012, up from $2.4 billion in 2006, according to iSuppli estimates.* "

This technology ecosystem, plus the extreme interest by companies in getting in on what is seen as the next wave of product innovation, practically guarantees that touchscreens and gestural interfaces will be entering the home and traditional office over the next several years.

SUPPLANTING THE DESKTOP METAPHOR?

Often when one mentions interactive gestures, the conversation turns to the impact that gestural interfaces will have on the desktop. Will the traditional keyboard-mouse-monitor setup be replaced by a touchscreen? Or a headset and special gloves?

The simple answer is…maybe, but probably not in the near future. It takes a long time for a technology, especially one as deeply ingrained as "traditional" computing, to be supplanted. Besides, a keyboard is still necessary for heavy data input (e.g., email, instant messaging, and word processing), although with a haptic system (see later in this chapter), this could be mitigated. The monitor (or some sort of visual display) is necessary as well, although this could easily be a touchscreen (as it is on some newer systems and on tablet PCs). The most vulnerable part of our existing PC setup is the mouse: the mouse could be replaced (and on many laptops it already has) by touchpads or a gestural means of controlling the cursor and other on-screen objects.

It certainly is possible that some jobs and activities that are currently accomplished using a traditional system will be replaced by a gestural interface. If you aren't doing heavy data entry, for instance, why do you need a keyboard and mouse? Gestural interfaces can and should be used for specialized applications and workstations.

The influence of interactive gestures will likely be felt, however, by the further warping—and even enhancement—of the desktop metaphor. If interactive gestures become one input device (alongside traditional keyboards and voice recognition), they could start to affect basic interactions with the PC. Waving

---

* "A Touching Story at CES," by Catherine Holahan, *BusinessWeek*, January 10, 2008. Read it online at *http://www.businessweek.com/technology/content/jan2008/tc2008019_637162.htm*.

a hand could move the windows to the side of the screen, for example. Finger flicks could allow you to quickly flip through files. Even a double head nod could open an application.

Figure 8-1. *DigiDesk, a touchscreen work space that utilizes advanced visualization and modeling of information, smarter integration of metadata, and more sophisticated pattern recognition. Courtesy Microsoft's Center for Information Work.*

The home, being semiprivate, may allow for a wider range of gestural products, since in the home you can do certain gestures and activities which you would seldom do in a workplace—for instance, clapping your hands to turn on a washing machine. Although gestural interfaces will naturally be used for "traditional applications" (already millions of people are using them with trackpads), they may find their greatest use in specialized applications and products.

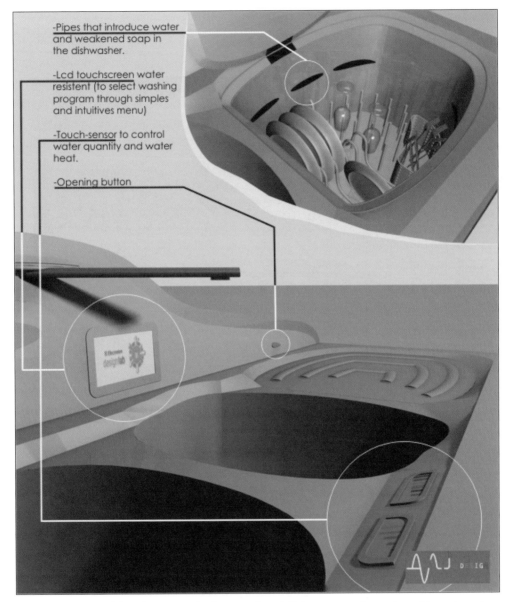

-Pipes that introduce water and weakened soap in the dishwasher.

-Lcd touchscreen water resistent (to select washing program through simples and intuitives menu)

-Touch-sensor to control water quantity and water heat.

-Opening button

Figure 8-2. *A dishwasher concept by Cristiano Giuggioli that uses an ultrasonic washing system. A water-resistant touchscreen allows users to plan washing programs and timers. Another touchscreen is on the edge of the sink to control the quantity and heat of the water. Courtesy Designboom.*

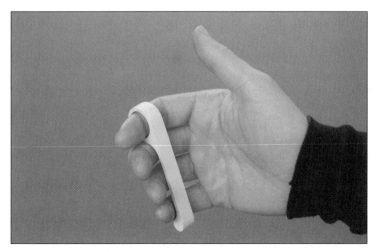

Figure 8-7. *The Spectacle of Paying attempts to make paying with e-money more physical through gestures. Users wear a sort of brass-knuckles device over their fingers and make visible gestures as a means of transferring and exchanging money face to face. Courtesy Gunnar Green.*

CONVERGENCE WITH OTHER TECHNOLOGIES

Few technologies live in isolation, and interactive gestures are no exception. In the future, the line between the following technologies and the world of interactive gestures will only grow blurrier as the technologies and systems grow closer together.

VOICE RECOGNITION

Once we move past just using a keyboard and mouse to interact with our digital devices, our voices seem like the next logical input device. Voice recognition combined with gestures could be a powerful combination, allowing for very natural interactions. Imagine pointing to an object and simply saying, "Tell me about this chair."

Using voice with gestures could also help overcome the limitations of modes using free-form gestures. Users could issue voice commands to switch modes, then work in the new mode with gestures.

VIRTUAL REALITY

Virtual reality (VR) is the technology that always seems on the edge of tomorrow, and gestures, once you are in an immersive space, are a likely way of navigating and controlling the virtual environment. After all, the cameras and projectors are possibly already in place to display the environment, and the user is likely wearing or using some sort of gear onto which other sensors can be placed.

UBIQUITOUS COMPUTING

Especially with patterns such as *Proximity Activate/Deactivate* and *Move Body to Activate*, interactive gestures encroach on the field known as **ubiquitous computing (ubicomp)**. Ubicomp envisions a world in which computing power has been thoroughly integrated into everyday objects and activities through sensors, networks, and tiny microprocessors. Ubicomp engages many computational devices and systems simultaneously as people go about their ordinary activities—people who may or may not be aware that they are users of a ubicomp system.

With its emphasis on integration with normal activities, interactive gestures are the natural partner to detect and use ubicomp systems. Ubicomp systems, with their ability to sense and distribute information, could be an enormous boon to gestural interfaces, performing activities such as importing personal gestural preferences to objects in any room you are in. Your touchscreen remote control in your hotel room could be exactly the same as yours at home. As you walk into another room of your house, ubicomp systems could dim lights in other rooms, IM your spouse to let her know where you are, and change the cushions on the sofa to reflect your desired firmness. But maybe you don't want any of that; with a gestural system in place, a wave of a hand could make you invisible to the system.

Because in physical spaces we're not typically without our bodies, using our bodies to control any ubicomp system around us seems like a natural pairing.

RADIO FREQUENCY IDENTIFICATION AND NEAR FIELD COMMUNICATION

More and more devices are being built that incorporate Near Field Communication (NFC) technology (a new standard based on RFID), and some manufacturers, such as Nokia, are enabling interactive gestures with their devices as a way of enabling NFC. NFC is a short-range, high-frequency wireless communication technology that enables the exchange of data among devices that are very close together—within 4 inches (10 cm). Since NFC requires the devices in question to be very close in physical proximity to communicate, a gesture such as tapping or swiping devices together is a natural way to trigger communication.[*] With NFC, users can do everything from sharing business cards and images with another device, to paying for a bus ticket, to using their mobile device as a sort of **universal controller** for all sorts of consumer devices that need a rich interface but don't have the physical form or price range to justify one.[†]

---

[*] The Touch Project at the Oslo School of Architecture and Design explores the intersection of NFC and gestures: *http://www.nearfield.org/*.

[†] See Christof Roduner's paper, "The Mobile Phone as a Universal Interaction Device—Are There Limits?" at *http://www.vs.inf.ethz.ch/publ/papers/rodunerc-MIRW06.pdf*.

Although the gestures for NFC are fairly limited to touches, taps, presses, and swipes, the use and position of these devices in an environment will have to be carefully designed.

NFC and RFID, once installed in objects and connected to the Internet (neither one a trivial task), will create what has been called *The Internet of Things*. Objects all over the environment will be equipped with sensors and RFID and/or NFC tags, allowing for communication about their location, creation, and history of use. How people interact with this Internet of Things has yet to be determined, but gestures, particularly gestures with smart objects, will likely play a part as readers, interpreters of data, and controllers.

GESTURING WITH SMART OBJECTS

Up until now, we've mostly discussed gestures in air or touches on screens, assuming that what we're gesturing with (if anything) is simply a "dumb," mostly mechanical device, perhaps filled with sensors, such as the Wiimote. But what if the devices we use are smart themselves—devices that change their functionality depending on the gestures made with them, or that use gestures in clever ways to make interactions subtler and more natural?

Figure 8-8. *The "Bar of Soap" is a prototype device that senses how it is being held and adjusts its functionality accordingly. It can "transform" into a phone, camera, game console, or PDA. Courtesy Brandon Thomas Taylor and MIT Media Lab.*

A Nokia marketing video[*] announcing the company's new (and as of this writing still unlaunched) S60 series phones with touchscreens contained one small moment, which designers have noted and commented on,[†] that demonstrates this well. In the (admittedly cheesy) video, a woman is talking to her boyfriend. On the table between them is her mobile phone (an S60 Touch of course!), its face up. The phone rings, and rather than interrupt her face-to-face conversation to fumble with the phone or ignore it until the call goes to voicemail (as we would have to do now), she simply flips it over, presumably sending the call to voicemail. It's a great example of a gesture taking on meaning via a smart device.

Figure 8-9. *In this demo, Microsoft's Surface recognizes the object sitting on it as a mobile phone and can pass information back and forth. Courtesy Microsoft.*

This gets us close to the related fields of haptic UIs and tangible UIs. **Haptic UIs** deliver feedback (in the form of vibrations, shakes, dynamic texture, temperature changes, etc.) that can be felt by touch alone. In fact, many feel that haptic UIs will eventually replace pure touchscreens because of their ability to create a more mechanical feeling (e.g., by creating buttons on the fly), which conveys more feedback to users than visuals or sound alone. And, although this author doesn't feel that pure touchscreens are going away anytime soon, haptics advocates do have a point: there is something more innately satisfying, more natural about the feeling of pushing a mechanical button than tapping a smooth surface. It is likely we will begin to see an integration of haptics with touchscreens, with haptic buttons appearing at specific times (as, for instance, for a keyboard).

Figure 8-10. *A prototype device using Nokia's "haptikos" technology. It is usually a standard touchscreen device with a smooth surface, but now the keyboard has a tactile feel when the keys are pressed and released, simulating the feeling of typing on an actual keyboard. Courtesy Nokia.*

Tangible UIs take a piece of data or functionality and embody it in a physical object that can then be manipulated manually. A classic example is Durrell Bishop's Marble Answering Machine (1992). In the Marble Answering Machine, a marble represented a single message left on an answering machine. Users dropped a marble into a dish to play back the associated message or return the call.

It's not much of a leap to imagine gestural systems in which users gesture with pieces of data. Rather than dropping a marble into a dish, for instance, users could tap the marble with a finger to hear the message or spin it to return the call.

The smarter our objects become, the more nuanced they can be about interpreting gestures. It's not hard to imagine your touchscreen laptop knowing when you are annoyed (because your taps are more abrupt and forceful) and adjusting accordingly.

Figure 8-11. *TangibleTable allows users to manipulate the display embedded into the table via different physical controls that are placed on the table's surface. Courtesy Daniel Guse and Manuel Hollert.*

Figure 8-13. *This "unicycle" cobot, consisting of a single wheel steered by a motor, demonstrates two essential control modes: "free" mode in which users can steer the wheel wherever they want, and "virtual surface" mode in which the cobot confines the user's motion to a software-defined guiding surface. Courtesy Northwestern McCormick School of Mechanical Engineering.*

Their use in particular environments (which could be equipped with sensors), plus the fact that they could be used for physical tasks that lend themselves to movement, make them perfect for extension by interactive gestures. Cobots augment human physicality, making us stronger, more accurate, and faster. Humans can do what they do best—human thought, problem solving, and skilled movements—while machines can do what they do best—more physical power and speed, and the ability to go into environments where it would be otherwise unsafe for people.

Imagine, for instance, a mechanic being able to lift and tilt a car with a gesture. Or a surgeon being able to make incredibly precise incisions and control tiny surgical cobots by touch alone.[*] Or musicians being able to play multiple instruments at once.

Even regular old robots are getting into interactive gestures. Aaron Powers, interaction designer at iRobot, hinted that even the humble floor cleaner Roomba might soon respond to gestures by its owner.[†] Other robots have been built that respond to clapping.

---

[*] See, for instance, "Restoring the Human Touch to Remote-Controlled Surgery," by Anne Eisenberg, in the *New York Times*, May 30, 2002. Found online at *http://biorobotics.harvard.edu/news/timesarticle.htm*.

[†] In "What Robotics Can Learn from HCI," ACM *interactions* Magazine, XV.2, March/April 2008.

GESTURES AS A DESIGN TOOL

In the movie *Iron Man* (2008), Tony Stark (played by Robert Downey, Jr.) manipulates in space a piece of the Iron Man armor he's designing. This sort of real-time manipulation of physical products—CAD coupled with 3D hologram imaging—would be a killer app for engineers, architects, and industrial designers alike, not to mention artists. It is difficult (and some would argue impossible) to design 3D objects well on a 2D medium such as a computer screen—or even paper, for that matter. Having the ability to prototype and manipulate objects in 3D space using interactive gestures would create an entirely new tool set for the creation of objects.

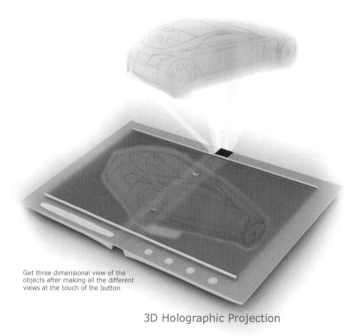

Get three dimensional view of the objects after making all the different views at the touch of the button

3D Holographic Projection

Figure 8-14. *This concept of a future touchscreen PC by Harsha Kutare and Somnath Chakravorti shows a possibility for using 3D projections as a design tool. Courtesy Microsoft and IDSA.*

Additionally, the ability to collaborate on tables and walls *digitally* but with the ease of analog methods such as whiteboards and paper—unencumbered by keyboards, mice, and the like—will be a tremendous boon to designers, and really to anyone. One only has to sit in a meeting filled with laptops whose screens become de facto barriers to see that other technology solutions would make the situation more collaborative and productive.

GESTURES FOR TOUCHSCREENS

These are common gestures used mainly on touchscreens and other interactive surfaces. To see these gestures in action, refer to Chapter 3.

TAP

The tip or pad of the finger touches the surface briefly (<100 milliseconds). A double tap performs this gesture twice rapidly, with a <75-millisecond pause in between the two contacts. Use for pushing buttons and selecting.

DRAG/SLIDE

The tip or pad of the finger moves over the surface without losing contact with the surface. Use for drag-and-drop and scrolling.

FLICK ("FLING")

Flick can be done in two ways. In the first way, the finger is crooked to start, and then the tip of the finger or part of the finger pad brushes the surface briefly (<75 milliseconds) as the finger uncurls. In the second way, the finger is straighter and the movement is nearly reversed, with the finger drawing closer to the body and the fingertip or part of the finger pad brushing the surface. Both of these are also called *Fling*. Use to quickly move objects, or to scroll.

NUDGE

The pad of a straight (index) finger slides briefly (<2 seconds) forward. Use to move objects.

PINCH

Two fingers (typically the thumb and index finger, although it can be two fingers from either hand or even two fingers on two different hands on multitouch surfaces) move closer together. Use for scaling.

SPREAD

Two fingers (typically the thumb and index finger, although it can be two fingers from either hand or even two fingers on two different hands on multitouch surfaces) move farther apart. Use for scaling.

HOLD

The tip or pad of the finger is pressed onto the surface for an extended period of time. Also called *Press*. Use for selection or extended scrolling.

GESTURES FOR FREE-FORM SYSTEMS

These are common gestures used mainly in environments and new devices. To see some of these gestures in action, refer to Chapter 4.

HEAD

HEAD COCKED

The head tilts to the left or right without turning.

Possible uses. Changing perspective on-screen; moving a cursor left or right.

TILT UP/DOWN

The whole head moves up or down but not up and down quickly (see *Nod Yes*).

Possible uses. Changing perspective on-screen; moving a cursor or slider up or down; flipping a switch; scrolling up/down.

TURN LEFT/RIGHT

The head turns so that the face becomes a profile and remains there (see *Shake No* for a similar movement).

Possible uses. Moving an avatar left or right; moving a cursor or slider left/right; scrolling left/right.

NOD YES

The head moves up and down in an affirmative movement. Note that this motion does not signify "yes" in certain parts of the world, such as the Middle East; in fact, it signifies the opposite.

Possible uses. Choosing an option; rapidly scrolling up/down.

SHAKE NO

The head shakes left and right as a negative gesture. Note that this motion does not signify "no" in certain parts of the world, such as the Middle East; in fact, it signifies the opposite.

Possible uses. Rejecting an option; rapidly scrolling left/right.

TORSO

STANDING

The body is in an upright position.

Possible uses. Returning to the default; changing modes (e.g., when shifting from sitting); turning on/off.

SITTING

The top half of the torso is erect while the legs are folded to accommodate resting on an object, such as a chair.

Possible uses. Changing modes (e.g., when shifting from standing); turning on/off.

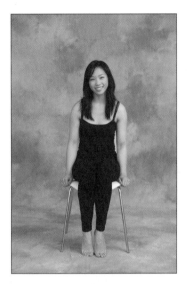

LAYING DOWN

The body is in a prone, horizontal position.

Possible uses. Changing modes (e.g., when shifting from standing); turning on/off.

RECLINING

The body is in a nearly horizontal position, with the top half at a slightly elevated angle.

Possible use. Changing modes (e.g., when shifting from standing).

TWIST LEFT/RIGHT

The top half of the body rotates left or right, turning at or near the waist.

Possible uses. Moving an avatar left or right; moving a cursor or slider left/right; scrolling left/right.

LEAN LEFT/RIGHT

The top half of the body tilts at an angle away from its midpoint to the left or right.

Possible uses. Moving an avatar left or right; moving a cursor or slider left/right; scrolling left/right.

BOW

The body bends forward at the waist.

Possible uses. Confirming or selecting a choice; moving an avatar forward.

HANDS ON HIPS

Hands are placed on the hips.

Possible uses. Stopping an action; pausing.

ON ALL FOURS

Person is on her hands and knees, low to the ground.

Possible uses. Lowering a setting; activating the lower portion of an area.

LEGS

LIFT STRAIGHT

A leg is raised forward.

Possible uses. Moving an avatar forward; selecting something on the lower part of a large screen.

KNEE COCKED

A single knee is lifted forward, raising the foot off the ground and bending the leg into roughly a 90-degree angle.

Possible use. Moving an avatar forward.

KNEELING

The torso is upright, with the person kneeling on her knees with her legs behind her.

Possible use. Lowering an object or avatar.

ON ONE KNEE

The torso is upright, with one leg in front, bent at the knee, while the other leg is also bent, resting on the knee with the lower leg behind.

Possible use. Lowering an object or avatar.

ON ONE LEG

One leg is lifted off the floor while the other remains on the floor.

Possible uses. Simple switching; left/right scrolling.

JUMP/HOP

One foot or both feet are lifted off the ground quickly.

Possible uses. Simple switching; selecting; clicking.

CROUCH

Both feet remain on the ground while the knees are bent and the torso is lowered.

Possible use. Lowering a setting (volume, lights, temperature, etc.).

LUNGE

One leg moves backward while the other bends into a 90-degree angle, causing the torso to lean forward.

Possible uses. Moving an avatar forward; changing the *z*-axis.

LIFT TO SIDE

A single leg lifts to the right or left while the foot remains facing forward. Typically the right leg lifts to the right, the left leg to the left.

Possible uses. Moving an avatar to the side; scrolling left/right.

LEG ANGLED OUT

While lifted, the leg and foot are at an angle less than 90 degrees.

Possible uses. Turning an avatar left/right, as a dial or slider position indicator.

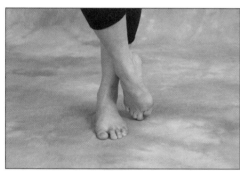

LEGS/ANKLES CROSSED

One leg goes over the other, at the ankle, calf, or knee.

Possible use. Stopping forward movement by an avatar.

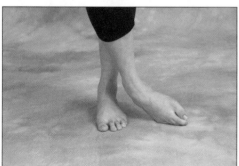

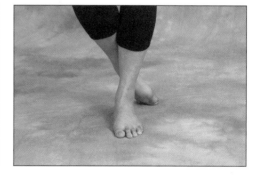

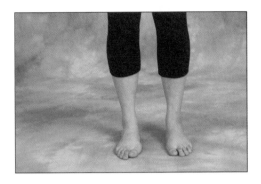

FEET

FLAT FOOT/STOMP

In this basic position, both feet are flat on the floor, pointed forward. Jumping turns this into a stomp, as does bringing a single foot up and down heavily.

Possible uses. Returning to a default position (from other foot positions); basic switching.

ANGLED UP

While the heel of the foot rests on the floor, the front of the foot angles up at a 45-degree angle.

Possible use. Stopping an action.

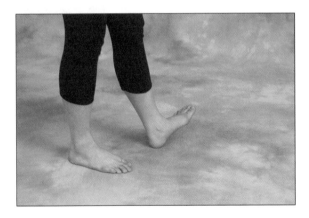

TIPTOE/TOE TAP

Only the toes are touching the floor; the rest of the foot is lifted off the floor.

Possible uses. Changing modes; switching on/off.

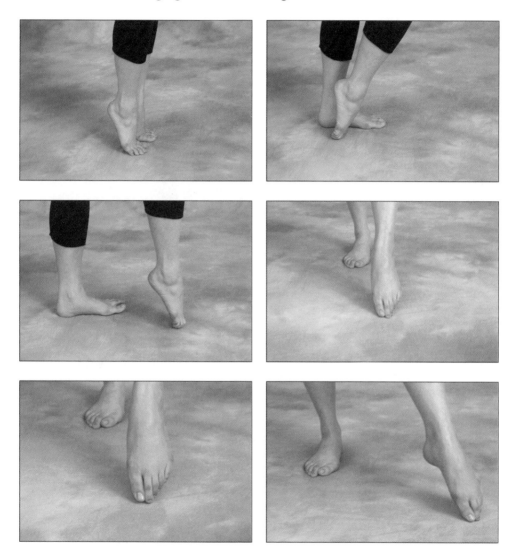

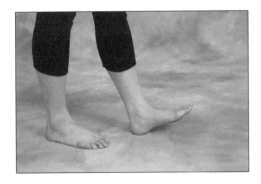

HEEL TO TOE OR BALL/TOE OR BALL TO HEEL

The foot tilts forward onto the toes or ball of the foot and then back onto the heel (or vice versa). Done rapidly, this creates a rocking motion with the foot.

Possible uses. Performing repetitive tasks; performing anything that requires rhythm; simple switching; moving an avatar forward.

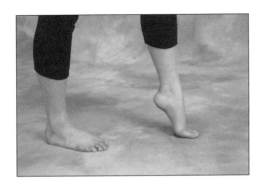

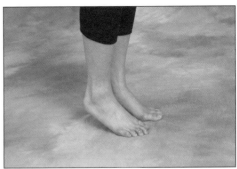

TURNED IN/OUT

The feet angle toward or away from the midline of the body.

Possible uses. Moving a slider or switch; changing on-screen perspective.

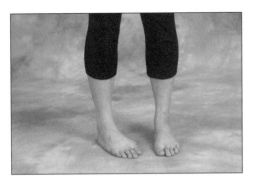

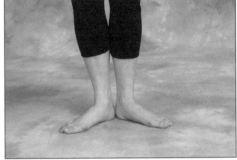

ARMS

ARM(S) DOWN

One arm or both arms are positioned straight down against the body.

Possible uses. Returning to a default position; deselecting; deactivating.

ARM(S) UP

One arm or both arms are raised straight up above the head.

Possible uses. Increasing a setting; activating objects above the head (e.g., lighting).

ARMS FOLDED

Both arms are folded across the chest.

Possible use. Stopping an action.

ARM(S) IN FRONT

One arm or both arms are lifted and extended straight forward, parallel to the floor.

Possible uses. Confirming or selecting a choice; moving an avatar forward; dragging and dropping.

SHH

A raised forefinger is pressed to the lips to indicate a need for quiet.

Possible uses. Muting sound; lowering volume.

COME HERE

A flat hand is angled toward the floor and then waved back and forth briskly.

Possible use. Moving an object (physical or digital) closer on the z-axis.

SHOO

A flat hand is angled toward the floor and then waved back and forth briskly.

Possible uses. Moving an object (physical or digital) away on the z-axis; canceling; quitting.

PUSH

One hand or both hands are flat and at a 90-degree angle to the floor, pointed upward and extended straight out from the body.

Possible uses. Moving an object (physical or digital) away on the z-axis; canceling; quitting.

PULL

With the hand(s) extended and palms up, the fingers curl toward the body and the arm bends at the elbow.

Possible use. Moving an object (physical or digital) closer on the *z*-axis.

FINGERS CROSSED

The forefinger and middle finger are extended, and the forefinger folds beneath the middle finger, forming an *X* shape.

Possible uses. Activating special actions; an alternative for tapping (when pressed on a surface).

STOP

A flat hand is held upward and forward, with the palm facing away from the body. Note that this is very offensive in some parts of the world, such as Greece.

Possible uses. Canceling; quitting.

SLAP

A flat hand is moved left/right in a sweeping motion. This can be fast or slow, mimed or real. If real, one side of the hand will strike a person or object.

Possible uses. Canceling; quitting; moving objects aside.

PALM UP/DOWN

One hand is flat and parallel to the floor, with the palm facing toward or away from the floor.

Possible uses. Receiving/rejecting a digital object; simple switching.

PINCH

The tips of the thumb and forefinger are brought together in a grasping motion.

Possible uses. Picking up objects; shrinking objects; collapsing menus.

CUP PALM

The hand is parallel to the floor, with the palm up and slightly curved so that the palm forms a bowl shape.

Possible uses. Opening; receiving information.

BLOWN KISS

Several fingertips are pressed to the lips and then flung outward, away from the body.

Possible uses. Selecting; closing.

TIP OF THE HAT

The person pantomimes the action of grasping the brim of a hat on her head, near the forehead, and tilting it forward.

Possible use. Activating.

HAND RUB

Both hands rub rapidly together to signify being cold and trying to warm up.

Possible use. Increasing temperature.

MONEY RUB

The thumb rubs against the forefinger and middle finger, with the pinky and ring finger curled, signifying money.

Possible use. Displaying a balance or total.

NOSE TAP

The tip of the forefinger is touched to the tip of nose, sometimes tapping multiple times, signifying "You are correct."

Possible uses. Selecting; confirming; activating.